Kenneth E. Eble

The Art of
Administration

>>>->>>->>>->>>->>>->>>->>>->>>->>>->>>->>>->>>->>>->>>->>>->>>->>>->>>

Jossey-Bass Publishers
San Francisco • Washington • London • 1978

THE ART OF ADMINISTRATION
A Guide for Academic Administrators
by Kenneth E. Eble

Copyright © 1978 by: Jossey-Bass, Inc., Publishers
433 California Street
San Francisco, California 94104
&
Jossey-Bass Limited
28 Banner Street
London EC1Y 8QE

Library of Congress Catalogue Card Number LC 78-62572

International Standard Book Number ISBN 0-87589-383-X

Manufactured in the United States of America

JACKET DESIGN BY WILLI BAUM

FIRST EDITION

Code 7823

The Jossey-Bass Series
in Higher Education

Preface

❯❯❯❯❯❯❯❯❯❯❯❯❯❯❯❯❯❯❯❯❯❯❯❯❯❯❯❯❯❯❯❯❯❯❯❯❯

This book is quite simply a handbook for administrators, particularly for those who are entering administration for the first time. I have chosen to call it the *art* of administration deliberately. College and university administrators, most of them former and future teachers and researchers, often take too little pride in successful administration and receive too little credit for administering well. If calling administration an art exalts the activity more than it deserves, it does so for good cause. Surely the complexities and subtleties of working with people, the skill and sensitivity necessary to doing it well, and the fulfillment of one's vision largely through other people deserve to be regarded as an art.

This book is a companion piece to my earlier book *The Craft of Teaching*. In calling administration an *art*, teaching a *craft*, I am not attempting to raise the status of administration above that of teaching, nor to shift attention away from the details vital to good administering. I wanted to call it "The Grubby Book," for that is often how both faculty and administrators think of administrative work, but other heads prevailed. The main point of the book is that good administration is very useful—if not essential—to good teaching, somewhat as good teachers are useful—if not essential—to good students. Both are useful to the advancing of knowledge and furthering of learning that define the ends of education.

Amidst the general outpouring of books on college and university administration, what purpose does another book serve? First, it serves the purpose of addressing many of the problems, vexations, frustrations, and satisfactions college administrators face. The point of view is personal but representative, I think, of faculty both drawn to and suspicious of administrative careers. Second, the book adopts a common tongue rather than the language of specialized scholarship. Increasingly, within the university, people don't speak the same language, adding to the difficulties faculty and administrators have in understanding each other. Third, as the book uses a common tongue, so I hope it addresses common purposes—not faculty against administrators nor administrators ruling over faculty but all working toward higher ends than daily chores often permit either to see. It places before all of us, whether our discipline is chemistry or education or English or business, a set of observations that may be useful to systematic efforts to prepare some of us for administering the important work in which we all are engaged.

This book makes no claim to explore the aims of higher education, or the current state of academic governance, or the ramifications of public support and financial planning and the like. Nor does it take up such important issues, both chronic and current, as the scarcity of women in administrative positions. Although its attention to the details of administration has wide application, no attempt is made to identify and discuss all the variety of managerial and supervisory activities to be found in academic bureaucracy. At its widest range, it gives advice to any individual expected to exercise administrative duties, but its examples and illustrations are drawn from the academic side of administration, and its aims are to keep the details of administrative functioning in close touch with scholarship and learning.

In preparing this book, I have had a chance to read and reread many books and articles dealing directly with college and university administration. I have even dared to use the title *The Art of Administration* and risk confusion with Ordway Tead's book of 1951. For that book, as excellent now as when it was written, surveys the art of administration from a perspective and toward ends different from mine. In addition, I have used the occasion to range outside higher education into the scholarly and professional literature of business management. To a humanist peering into another discipline, it was a pleasure to find so much human concern manifested there. The bringing to bear of behavioral science upon business management and the current emphasis upon the human dimensions of management seem as natural as they appear to be fruitful.

I hope I have used this material well. For, though it has as many dreary patches as the literature of any field, it has its moments of enlightenment, too. One might as accurately be describing a novel as describing a sober book on management—Chris Argyris' *Management and Organizational Development*—in a sentence that reads (1971, pp. xiii–xiv): "The book is filled, perhaps repetitively so, with struggle, conflict, groping, bewilderment, anger, frustration, and above all the continual amazement and dismay of the participants."

Most of the material in this book comes from personal experience. Almost half of my twenty-five years as a college professor have been spent in administrative positions, and seldom during the other half have I been able to keep from observing administrators or from pondering the effects of administration. Long before that, my coping with education administration began with the desperate need to convince a junior high school principal that writing *shit* on the school sidewalk was not a capital offense. This book is a plea to all administrators to believe that the business of life is more important than the management of personnel, that civility and compassion

are as important to administering as regulating and enforcing, and
that one can find in administration joy, or, if not that, the great
satisfactions that come from being able to contribute to the joys
and satisfactions of others.

Salt Lake City, Utah   KENNETH E. EBLE
August 1978

Contents

➤➤➤➤➤➤➤➤➤➤➤➤➤➤➤➤➤➤➤➤➤➤➤➤➤➤➤➤➤➤➤

5. Planning   54

6. Keeping Sane   70

7. Getting the Most Out of People   80

8. Identifying Administrators   90

9. Selecting Faculty   102

10. Serving and Leading   113

11. Making Decisions   126

12. Complex Skills for Complex Tasks   137

     References   150

     Index   157

The Author

➤➤➤-➤➤➤-➤➤➤-➤➤➤-➤➤-➤➤➤-➤➤➤-➤➤➤-➤➤➤-➤➤➤-➤➤➤-➤➤-➤➤➤-➤➤➤-➤➤➤-➤➤➤-➤➤➤

KENNETH E. EBLE is professor of English and University Professor at the University of Utah, Salt Lake City. He received his B.A. and M.A. degrees from the University of Iowa (1948, 1949) and his Ph.D. degree in English from Columbia University (1956).

    Eble began teaching at Upper Iowa University in 1949 and also taught at the Columbia School of General Studies (1951–54) and Drake University (1954–55) before joining the faculty at the University of Utah in 1955. He has served as visiting professor in American studies at Carleton College (1967) and directed seminars in college teaching for the Colombian Ministry of Education (1975) and the Kansas City Regional Council for Higher Education (1976).

From 1964 to 1969, he was chairman of the English department at the University of Utah, taking leave from 1969 to 1971 to direct the Project to Improve College Teaching, cosponsored by the American Association of University Professors (AAUP) and the Association of American Colleges (AAC) and funded by the Carnegie Corporation. In 1973, he was awarded an honorary Doctor of Humane Letters from Saint Francis College (Biddeford, Maine) and was Distinguished Visiting Scholar for the Educational Testing Service in 1973–1974.

During the past ten years, Eble has frequently been a guest speaker and consultant on teaching and faculty development at more than 150 colleges and universities in the United States and Canada. He has served in many official positions within the AAUP, the Modern Language Association, the National Council of Teachers of English, and Phi Beta Kappa.

Eble's writing has embraced not only education but American literature, the humanities, history of ideas, and popular culture. In addition to *Professors as Teachers* (1972) and *The Craft of Teaching: A Guide to Mastering the Professor's Art* (1976), Eble's books include *F. Scott Fitzgerald* (rev. ed. 1976), *The Profane Comedy* (1962), *A Perfect Education* (1966), and, as editor, *Howells: A Century of Criticism* (1962) and *The Intellectual Tradition of the West* (1967).

In addition to consulting, writing, and teaching a full schedule of classes, Eble plays tennis year-round, hikes in the mountains in summer, and skis in winter. He and his wife, Peggy, who is involved in local government and civil rights activities, have two sons and a daughter.

The Art of Administration

A Guide for
Academic Administrators

Chapter 1

>>>->>>->>>->>>->>>->>>->>>->>>->>>->>>

Exploring the Territory

>>>->>>->>>->>>->>>->>>->>>->>>->>>->>>->>>->>>->>>->>>->>>

Simon Suggs, one of the craftiest rascals to be found in American frontier humor, lived by the motto, "It is good to be shifty in a new country." Simon's shrewd ability to feel out a new territory was a necessity for survival on the American frontier; being quick on one's feet and adept at sizing up friend and foe may be as useful to professors newly arrived at administration. Some administrators, as I have observed them, combine boldness with dexterity. But boldness is less common than cautious shrewdness, well short of that kind of resourcefulness which both expands frontiers and builds superior institutions.

The ability of college professors—for almost no one else becomes an academic administrator—to adapt to new responsibilities covers a range of adaptive behavior, from the general equivocation with which administration is regarded to specific evasions that go with trying to please one's administrative superiors and former colleagues. Administrators may not practice shiftiness

1

by nature, but academic life is often intensely political and tact
and diplomacy are necessary, even as they may be hard to distinguish from subterfuge and guile. Administrators who are too
shifty are commonly judged harshly. But those may serve no better
who lack quickness and flexibility.

Regarding administration as too new a country also has
adverse effects. It increases the seeming separation of the academic
from the administrative when they are actually and necessarily
intertwined. It magnifies the distances between an administrator and
former faculty colleagues which increase over time and as one rises
in the administrative ranks. It can result in faculty and administration occupying separate territories, each jealous of its rights and
seldom hospitable even to friendly visits. All of these are reasons
for urging faculty members who enter administration to do so in a
more roguish spirit, to set out with a spirit of adventure, and to
keep in touch with the folks back home.

If we are to have institutions that provide experiences con-
sonant with the high expectations of each year's students, administration must see itself, too, as an exciting and renewing experience.
And if the frontiers of knowledge are to exist as more than university rhetoric, administrators must have a part in creating and sus-
taining a climate which has something of the openness, daring, and
boisterousness even of the frontier.

These preliminary remarks are part of this chapter's intent
to set forth some of the major concerns of this book and to indicate
its organization, tone, and emphasis. The attitudes that individuals
hold toward administration and the climate of opinion that in-
fluences administrative conduct are obviously important. The personal qualities of administrators and the skills they acquire are worth
much examination. The carrying out of routine tasks without im-
pairing one's ability to realize larger aims is an inescapable duality
of administrative work. Resourcefulness may be the quality most
necessary to effective daily operations. Firm principles as to what
administration at its highest can accomplish underlie the realization
of larger aims.

The root and body of the word *administer* is *to serve*. Within
colleges and universities, that simple, vital meaning is often ob-
scured. Faculty and students are not easy constituencies to

serve, and governing boards, sources of support, and
alumni have their own ideas about administrative service.
Administrative structures stand uneasily between a hierarchical
model, in which one person serves another in a pyramid of
authority, and the model of shared governance, in which chronic
uneasiness exists about who serves whom. Neither individuals
nor structures have met the array of administrative problems
created by the diverse services expected of higher education institutions, particularly those very large institutions that characterize our
higher education system.

In the abstract, most faculty and administrators recognize
they are in service to others: to students and colleagues, to institutional and disciplinary aims, and to ideals that embrace both future
and past. But in the daily functioning of an institution the ideals
of service and the power to motivate actions may operate at a low
level. Raising that level might begin by renewing the concept of
college administrators as public servants and administration as
public service. Peter Caws, in *The Bankruptcy of Academic Policy*
(1972, p. 10), writes: "The *raison d'être* of all the institutions of a
democratic society is the service of the people. . . . Insofar as the
university is an institution of its society, its responsibility is to ask
itself how it can best serve the people." The prime responsibility
of an administrator may be to ennoble and invigorate the idea of
service and to handle the minute and multitudinous details through
which others may serve and be served.

There is a paradox here. The acts of leadership may at a
glance seem contrary to those of service. The attributes of one who
leads forcefully may seem at odds with the ideals of service. Yet the
paradox diminishes if one views teaching and learning—the principal justification for having college administrators—as intimately
related activities. Teaching and learning are not acts in which one
person in authority exercises power over another. They are acts in
which teacher and learner serve each other, both contributing to
the *leading out* that is the root meaning of the word *education*.

Robert Greenleaf has devoted his recent book, *Servant
Leadership*, to the many complexities that reside in *leading* and
serving. His concerns (1977, pp. 5–6) are "for the individual in
society and his seeming bent to deal with the massive problems of

our times wholly in terms of systems, ideologies, and movements"
and "for the individual as a serving person and the tendency to
deny wholeness and creative fulfillment to oneself by failing to lead
when there is the opportunity." He argues (1977, p. 7) that *"the
great leader is seen as servant first"* and that the real contradictions
that exist between serving and leading are resolved in the presence
and acts of truly successful leaders, not only in education but in
all our institutions.

Greenleaf's words state well the overarching premise on
which this book proceeds. The harmonizing of the ideals of serving
and leading is no less important than the daily carrying out of
acts that both serve and lead. College professors are jealous of their
independence, proud of their specialized competences, not easily
led, and suspicious of being told what or how they serve. And yet,
I think the commitment to college teaching begins in a sense of
service. However experience and conditions may dull that sense, it
is rarely altogether dimmed. Faculty members remain responsive to
signs that important services are being rendered—both from their
own teaching and research and from the institutions they are part
of. And since their attention is most often focused upon serving the
aims of learning in specific contexts, they may welcome leadership
that helps make their efforts a part of the larger service.

All administrators share in these responsibilities for both
serving and leading. Department heads, chairpersons, and directors
of the smaller academic divisions have particular responsibilities.
Because they work directly with faculty and students, they are key
figures in how an institution actually functions as a center of learning. Roach (1976, p. 13) estimates that 80 percent of all administrative decisions take place at the department level. Furthermore, this
level is also the entry level for most academic administrators, though
in large universities service in subordinate administrative jobs within
a department or division may precede chairing a department or
directing a division. A comprehensive survey of deans (Gould,
1964, p. 94) revealed that 64 percent of them were chairpersons
before they became deans. Experience in a deanship figures prom-
inently in the qualifications for higher academic positions.

Attention given to the lowest level of administration in this
book is therefore applicable to administrative functioning and to

considerations of leadership and service at all levels. The separate chapters do not attempt to define a chairperson's specific duties or the role of deans, vice-presidents, or presidents. Useful literature exists on all these subjects. For example, books by Gould (1964) and Dibden (1968) include formal studies of the academic dean-ship, anecdotal material and reminiscences, and thoughtful opinion pieces. Extensive bibliographies are to be found in both books. The department chairmanship has been less studied, but Brann and Emmet (1972) have compiled a useful set of readings growing out of a series of in-service institutes for chairpersons from 1969 to 1971. Eells and Hollis' annotated bibliography of the college presidency (1961) runs to 129 pages; their 1960 annotated bib-liography of administration of higher education runs to 370 pages and 2,708 items.

This literature defining the various roles and responsibilities of college administrators is supported by an even larger literature in the general field of administration and management. Drucker (1970, p. 149), writing in 1958, noted that "the literature of busi-ness management, confined to a few 'how to do' books only fifty years ago, has grown beyond any one man's capacity even to catalogue it." That abundance has been catalogued, however, and any college administrator or would-be administrator can go to the library and browse for months, years even, among the many books, carefully organized into dozens of categories, all having to do with administration. Books on various aspects of college and university administration are a large category in themselves.

Little in the contents of these books, however—perhaps somewhat more in the periodical literature—concerns itself with details of administration, with *how* administrators might carry out their many duties and responsibilities. Because of this lack, this book places its emphasis upon what I shall call the *functional* as against the *substantive* aspects of university administration. The substantive are those large, important matters everyone in academia deals with, most often in the abstract: the aims of higher education, or the current state of academic governance, or the ramifications of public support and financial planning, or the upgrading and maintaining of standards, and the like. The functional tend to be the dirty work: the engagement with getting things done and attending to details through which others are assisted in performing their jobs.

As leading and serving are vitally intertwined, so are the substantive and functional aspects of administration. Successful administrators have to keep in mind the lofty aims that reside in teaching and learning but bend to carrying out humble tasks that assist others in realizing these aims. The first five chapters of this book are firmly focused upon administrative details, small and large, often the hardest part of administrative work to face and yet both vital and unavoidable. The last chapters focus upon getting the most out of people, the most demanding and most rewarding of an administrator's tasks.

How successful an administrator is in working with others depends greatly upon the administrator's understanding of the psychic as well as material needs that motivate human beings. Success in understanding others begins with understanding oneself. Inasmuch as certain individuals are given large responsibilities for furthering and giving coherence to the work of others, they must be extraordinarily aware of their own motivations and sources of satisfactions, the nature and effects of their own ego drives among the ego drives of others. "We convince by our presence," Whitman wrote. McGregor's *The Human Side of Enterprise* (1960) may be the best of the books, by now dozens in number, that apply behavioral science and humanistic perspectives to the behavior of administrators. This persuasive body of theory and closely examined practices applies as fully to college administration as to business management. It applies with particular force to the constant interactions among members of a group trying to carry out a complex and important *human* enterprise.

As defining the focus and limiting the scope of this book have created problems of emphasis and organization, so has the subject matter created problems of striking the right tone. It is easy for faculty members to be satirical about college and university education. It is almost impossible for them not to be critical of administrators. Max Marshall, a microbiologist, son of a dean, and faculty member under sixteen deans, strikes a familiar satiric tone. "It is high time," he writes, in "How to Be a Dean" (1956, p. 636), "that someone told deans how to play their roles. Except the deans themselves, everyone knows how to be a dean, but nobody is sufficiently forthright to say so in public, permitting existing deans to get at the rules or coming deans to learn the art." Deans seem to take a disproportionate amount of abuse, from John Ciardi's "Education is too important a business to be left to deans" (Dibden, 1968, p. 185) to the anonymous definition of a dean as a person too dumb to be a professor and too smart to be president. Another jibe covers a wider territory: "The faculty's job is to think for the university, the president's to speak for it, and the dean's to make sure that the faculty doesn't speak or the president think."

As much as I am attracted to the spirit and tone of such utterances, I have chosen to temper my own satirical bent. At the same time, I have not backed away from drawing upon personal experience nor from employing the first person pronoun as it seemed useful. Thoreau spoke best on this matter. "In most books," he writes at the beginning of *Walden*, "the *I*, or first person, is omitted; in this it will be retained; that, in respect to egotism, is the main difference. We commonly do not remember that it is, after all, always the first person that is speaking." As regards this book, the use of the first person is a decided aid to clear and direct expression as well as an assertion that someone is taking responsibility for what is being said.

Ideally, presidents and deans and faculty should all think and speak and act wisely. And, though there is no sure path of development to those ends, surely there should be more definable means of preparing and training college administrators than now exist. Thomas Emmet (Brann and Emmet, 1972) claims to have established the first consulting firm presenting in-service institutes to middle management and faculty in higher education in 1967. My examination of the literature identified an Institute for Administrative Officers in Higher Education at the University of Chicago in 1923, though it was restricted to college presidents, deans, and personnel officers. The Phillips Foundation Program of Internships in Academic Administration began only in 1962; the American Council on Education's Academic Administration Internship Program in 1964 (Phillips, 1969). Sally Gaff (1978) sums up the present situation thus: "Most [college and university administrators] have not been trained in the skills demanded of them as educational executives; they have neither planned for careers in administration nor studied others functioning successfully in similar roles." Warren Bennis (1973), an authority on organizational development and former president of the University of Cincinnati, comments: "I am more and more impressed with the almost total lack of any rational career plan for academic administrators. Most of us got into this work adventitiously, and most of us do what we have either observed others do when they were in these roles or emulate, incorrectly, some other shadowy figures of the past, fantasies of Harvard Business School products, General Patton, creatures of fiction or movies, or some atavisms of leadership and authority which never were."

Although, as Bennis points out, academic administrators acquire skills in various ways both before and after assuming administrative positions, little of that development comes from systematic preparation or in-service training. Some explanation must be sought for the neglect in providing such preparation for administrators within the universities themselves (a similar neglect is apparent in the preparation of college teachers). For the universities are the prime source of research, study, and programs of preparation for both teaching in the public schools and education and business administration.

Not so for either college teaching or college administration, though there have been sporadic movements in both these directions. The reasons are complex. One is to be found in the attitudes and practices that separate academic disciplines from colleges of education and that separate liberal arts colleges from colleges of business. Formal higher education has long maintained a distinction between theoretical and practical studies, between those supported by academic tradition and those that have arrived later on the academic scene. The movement of normal schools and teacher's colleges and commercial colleges and business institutes into the universities has not brought an end to these value distinctions. I think they play a part in the lack of development of graduate work aimed specifically at acquiring skill in either college teaching or administration.

One other partial explanation may be offered, this one closely related to the idea that successful administration is rooted in the personality and character of the administrator. Perhaps the resistance to formal training for college teaching and administration arises from the adult's resistance to any learning that intrudes upon areas of the psyche close to the centers of personality and character. We are curious enough about these matters—the self-help book is a staple among best sellers through the ages—but we would have our curiosity satisfied by *self*-help. We resist the systematic efforts of *others* to shape our personalities by presuming to teach us how to perform such personal tasks as teaching or administering among our peers.

That teachers are systematically trained for the lower schools and administrators for both the schools and business does not destroy my hypothesis. In both instances, those in charge of training programs clearly separate themselves from those being trained, operating as professors in disciplines and institutions at considerable distance from both public schools and business establishments. Preparation of college teachers and administrators threatens to bring the professors who do it into too close contact with their own practices. Whatever explanations may be offered, the fact remains that in most universities neither the college of education nor the college of business plays a large role in preparing college teachers or administrators.

There are signs that the situation may be changing. Higher education as a field of specialization has developed greatly in the past twenty years, and administration tends to be a strong emphasis within that field. The demand for and opportunities in academic administration are probably greater today than demands and opportunities for faculty. Administrative development currently appears to be getting almost as much attention as faculty development. The growth of a literature in itself argues that the colleges and universities may begin to make more purposeful use of it in the preparation and in-service training of administrators.

A problem that still looms large is that the entry into academic administration is almost exclusively through the academic disciplines, most of which remain untouched by any but experiential knowledge of administration. I am not advocating systematic training programs—either for college teachers or administrators—that model themselves upon the kind of course work, independent study, and research that defines present graduate programs, both inside and outside colleges of education and business. What might better serve would be the bringing together of expertise and common sense of both the academic disciplines and the college of education or business. Theory and practice could be related as they rarely are within an academic department. Learning would not be terminal but ongoing, not from professor to student but toward the development of both.

Precisely, I suggest a "center" (to choose a neutral term) for university teaching and administration, which would draw faculty from both the academic disciplines and the ranks of administrators, for terms of perhaps one to three years. The whole operating faculty could be so chosen as to comprise at any one time a sufficient body of outlooks and competences and energies and enthusiasms to undertake a number of important learning and teaching responsibilities now not being attempted or carried out very well. One of these responsibilities would be the design and carrying out of programs of training for prospective college teachers and administrators. Such programs would draw upon the teaching within the separate departments that many Ph.D. candidates now do, enlarge the opportunities for administrative work as both a source of student financial support and future professional preparation, and enhance teaching and administration internally at the same time they were developing competence for future service elsewhere. Such programs would make more use of research and practice going on in colleges of education and business, as both are professionally concerned and in a scholarly way with teaching and administering.

I am not proposing a research center, though a number of these have made substantial contributions to both university teaching and administration. And I am specifically staying away from endorsing an expansion of graduate work in education into "higher education administration" modeled on traditional lines. The features that I see as important are not commonly found. The faculty would be drawn from the university and much of it, perhaps all, would not be permanently attached. It would be as much a learning faculty as a teaching faculty. Degrees might be offered but they would be both within a discipline and aim at developing competences beyond disciplines. And the degree-granting function might well be less important than the internal development of excellence in teaching and administration within the university at large. Research and expertise would be more applied from other disciplines than generated within the center. The realities of university teaching and administration and the capacities of a *university* to develop excellence in both would be guiding principles.

Finally, higher education since World War II has been characterized by continuing demands of the faculty for a larger part in the administration of the university. Within those areas specifically concerned with academic programs, faculties have gained great power, in part at the cost of assuming more administrative responsibilities. The movement away from administrative "heads" holding lifetime appointments to those who serve for only limited terms has increased the demand for administrators at all levels. Then, too, present conditions seem to have increased administrative turnover; administrators may wear out more quickly now than in the past.

More faculty members, therefore, will have to face the self-development and acquiring of attitudes and skills that go with being effective administrators. At the heart of that development must be a responsiveness to service, a willingness to lead, a capability for taking care of details, a firmness in holding on to higher goals, an ability to marshall successfully one's own energies, and an ability to make the most of the work of others. What Philip Selznick (1957, p. 4) has said of business executives applies as much to university administrators: "The executive becomes a statesman as he makes the transition from administrative management to institutional leadership." Human beings, including college faculty, do not resent leadership, even as they may despair over fumbling and bristle at manipulation or coercion. Statesmanlike leadership as such statesmanlike leadership should be exercised at all levels of university administration. Higher education cannot carry out any fraction of the many expectations heaped upon it without having leaders who inspire confidence in their largeness of mind and trust in their ability to assist others in reaching worthy goals.

>>>->>>->>>->>>->>>->>>->>>->>>->>>

Chapter 2

Getting Things Done

->>>->>>->>>->>>->>>->>>->>>->>>->>>->>>->>>->>>->>>->>>->>>->>>->>>->>>

By temperament, a successful administrator must be willing and able to deal with the dirty work. Within the body of a successful administrator should be the soul of a masterful file clerk, a consummate bookkeeper, a gem in the shipping room. If that soul only feeds upon fitting things into boxes and getting the mail out on time, its possessor may never get out of the shipping room. But the handling of small details in any art is directly connected with realizing great visions. As Conrad (1951, xxxix) said of fiction, its attainments as an art rest upon "an unremitting, never-discouraged care for the shape and ring of sentences." So with administering. Given the fact that any complex enterprise involves endless detail, successful administration requires the will both to embrace detail effectively and to resist being swallowed up by it.

However some administrators may chafe at being on the daily treadmill of getting things done, all administrators have to find ways of attending to the daily work. The eminent manage-

ment consultant Peter Drucker (1966) singles out managing one's
time as "everybody's number one problem." Drucker's response to
the problem begins with the systematic management of a person's
working hours. He claims that he has seldom found "a senior officer
who controls as much as 25 percent of his time" and advocates as a
first step toward increasing the "discretionary time" at one's disposal
the keeping of a written record of how time is actually spent. From
examining such a log critically, the administrator may find answers
to these important questions: (1) "What am I doing that really
does not need to be done at all—by me or anyone else?" (2)
"Which of the activities on my time log could be handled by some-
body else just as well, if not better?" and (3) "What do I do that
wastes the time of others?"

Drucker's observations are worth heeding. Everyone con-
tends in one way or another with the problem of getting things
done. My own experience leads me to make some practical suggestions here, in the form of nine propositions. I shall call them axioms,
for they are, like mathematical axioms, "assumed without proof
for the sake of studying the consequences."

Axiom One. *The way to big accomplishments is through
painstaking attention to small details.*

Many new administrators make their first mistakes in over-
looking the importance of handling details, doing or failing to do
seemingly unimportant things that turn out to have surprising and
often dismaying consequences. And many an administrator's vision
of large accomplishments is never realized because of general in-
eptness in taking care of details.

Let me illustrate these contentions, first with a story of a
new department chairman who made the mistake of looking at the
budget and reacting with panic. His first move was to institute a
number of petty economies, beginning with an attack on faculty
use of supplies. He did not realize that an attack on supplies does
not inflict minor damage to the capillaries; it is an assault on the
arteries. Focusing on the faculty's easy access to the supply room,
the chairman acted to put supplies under lock and key. A file
cabinet with a lock was all that was necessary, but, unfortunately,
the department had no such equipment, and the chairman called
maintenance to put a lock on an existing file. The ways of any

of the supporting agencies of a university can be mysterious, if not malevolent. Installing a cheap locking device on a steel filing cabinet posed an interesting problem: how to do it simply but as conspicuously as possible. The solution was admirable: a five-foot steel bar run from bottom to top through the handles, bent over the top, fashioned into a hasp, and secured by a bulldog padlock. It was crude and serviceable. It saved supplies; it fired passions. It became known as "the chairman's shaft," identified by the sign of the finger. It caused a mild uprising among the faculty, the dissolution of the secretary who had to dole out the paper clips, and impairment of the chairman's functions for most of the year. If one wanted to extract two specific lessons from this experience, one might be "Never mess with supplies as a way of saving money" and the other "Never take away small privileges that the past has freely bestowed." The general lesson is the one being elaborated here: the importance of seemingly small things.

The other illustration is of a department chairman's failing to carry out a small but necessary detail, perhaps because he didn't recognize its importance. The failure was in not appointing long-established department committees, for no apparent reason. The chairman was an amiable fellow and the department not inclined toward putting its administrators under much pressure. Unfortunately, the department was also one in which the main business had long been handled by committees. Restiveness grew. Relief that some department members felt in not being on committees was offset by anxieties arising from many matters not being taken care of. The chairman never did face an obvious responsibility squarely; instead, he kept promising to select committees and never did. In time, the chairman was not reappointed, largely because of his general inability to handle details. It is a fair guess that he may still feel that committee appointments were not all that important.

Axiom Two. *Sorting out what there is to do is a first step toward getting it done.*

Call them priorities, objectives, first things first—the identifying of things to be done is a fundamental concern for a new administrator and one that will continue to require a high degree of alertness. My emphasis is still upon the small things here, upon looking at a given task in terms of the various administrative details that will have to be handled if the job is to be done. It is pointless to engage in internal arguments about how such details stand in the way of getting at the important things. "The only common element in the deanship everywhere," Gould writes (1964, p. 10), "is a heavy work load complicated by a 'multitude of administrative fussiness.' It is this constant demand for attention to endless detail that vitiates the dean's energy and subverts his will to provide leadership."

The studies in Gould's book inventory some of the many routine tasks expected of an academic dean or chairperson. "In terms of time spent," McGrath writes (Gould, 1964, vii), "the deans place routine administrative duties at the top of their list of activities: correspondence, scheduling, catalogue, reports, and questionnaires." From my own experience as a department chairman, I would add details of budget and of promotion and tenure procedures, announcements, and memos, telephone queries and responses, matters of physical space and equipment and their upkeep, and numerous small interruptions that must be dealt with daily.

Keeping track of how one spends one's time, as Drucker has suggested, would probably lead to a longer and more carefully analyzed list. But giving priority to any of these details raises a perplexing problem. In working with routine matters that affect other people, ordinary setting of priorities doesn't apply. No one thing on any given day may be a first thing. In the minds of the people with whom a dean or department chairperson works, there may be a great many "first" concerns. When the administrator's sense of what is important coincides with the faculty's, harmony follows. When it doesn't, frictions arise.

Fortunately, most institutions set some simple priorities by establishing a calendar of administrative deadlines. The wise administrator should meet them, not because they reflect judgment and consideration but because fussing about them, delaying response, and eventually and tardily meeting them simply take too much energy. So that can be set as a simple priority: adhering to the administrative calendar. Doing that, an administrator might find more time to complain about deadlines, suggest modifications in the calendar, and work against bureaucratic busy-work.

Axiom Three. *Dealing with people is more taxing and time-consuming than dealing with things.*

In setting priorities, clearly dealing with people should have a high and privileged place. Yet, just as the handling of small details has much to do with large accomplishments, so does the handling of most administrative routines affect other people. Even simple acts such as choosing one's own office furniture or deciding to eat lunch at one's desk have an impact on the people one works with. A faculty handbook at Penn. State, for example, tries to identify all the duties of deans or department chairpersons. It lists nine "administrative" tasks, along with ten under the heading "faculty," three under "students," three under "promotion and liaison," and two additional categories, "committees" and "professional standing" (Brann and Emmet, 1972, pp. 7–10). Almost all the items in this staggering list involve working directly with other people.

In the face of such demands, an administrator may find it hard to escape feeling that other people are the main impediment to getting things done. Some faculty member always seems to want to talk about something; students keep showing up with problems; colleagues are getting married or divorced or facing other crises. Whole days get taken up with such matters. The best course is to acknowledge the vexations and to fight against regarding people as wasters of one's valuable time. Expect interruptions, face the most trivial of interruptions with equanimity, and allow for the time they will take. Any other course is fatal. Irritation only fosters counter-irritation, impatience another's impatience, temporizing another's inclination to temporize. Forthrightness and courtesy can work together, helping others not to waste their time but still creating a feeling that the administrator's time is at their disposal.

Axiom Four. *Doing the things you don't want to do first can save the day for things you can do with enthusiasm and satisfaction.*

The first purposeful act toward getting things done should be directed toward doing unpleasant tasks quickly and routinely. For example, I did not like the telephone when I came into administration, either my calling on it or its summoning me. Nevertheless, as an administrator, I concluded that making calls, disagreeable ones or not, first thing in the morning was a way of reducing psychic drain the rest of the day. It also reduced the number of calls likely to interrupt me at other times. Establishing a disagreeable task as a routine operation moved it toward being an automatic physical act rather than one involving conscious and vexing decisions.

Many disagreeable tasks are not routine matters. Dealing with the budget, a curse to many deans and department chairpersons, is both important and full of consequential details. Nevertheless, confronting the budget head-on, like making calls early, is preferable to putting it off. The sooner and more efficiently done, the more time left for confronting such vital educational matters as developing teaching competence in the faculty or raising the level of students' commitment to learning.

Some of the most disagreeable of administrative tasks are those that require confronting colleagues. The confrontation may be over scheduling, or not finding a parking place, or a memo misunderstood or one understood very clearly, or a squeaking chair, or the absence of coffee in the lounge. Or it may be one of a series of confrontations emerging out of an individual's personal distrust, or out of a personal or drinking problem, or out of loss of confidence or illness. Minor problems should not be confused with serious impairments; but both have to be faced. Better to get a colleague's irritations expressed, if not resolved on the spot, than to let them be held in and allowed to fester. The exactly right time to confront the more serious problems may never come, but an administrator's established willingness to deal with uncomfortable matters may be the best way of bringing a person to confront the problem, to seek help, and perhaps take some steps toward a solution.

Axiom Five. *A job assigned may not be a job well done.*

The best way of disposing of disagreeable tasks may seem to be to assign them to someone else. But that may not be a way of getting them done. A disagreeable task to one person may be just as disagreeable to and just as likely to be put off by another. While it is generally good advice for an administrator to decide which of many responsibilities can be carried out as well by others, such decisions must be made with care. It is too humanly inviting to get out from under disagreeable jobs by shifting them to others. The assigning of detail work to subordinates may be a genuine way of freeing oneself for important duties, or it may be an avoidance that seriously impairs one's overall functioning. An administrator must be wary of making lesser jobs unattractive to faculty and nonfaculty personnel alike, thus reducing the likelihood of their being done well. As to personal responsibilities for details, an administrator must chart a course between seeing that they are well taken care of by someone else and staying close enough to routine operations to keep informed and competent.

It takes time and close association to develop personnel to whom routines can be assigned with no further attention to their being done well. In the course of ordinary operations, monitoring, evaluating, or accounting for the work of others is an unavoidable part of getting things done. Establishing clear expectations as to performance is essential. Setting reasonable deadlines is often a part of setting expectations. Not letting expectations or deadlines go unobserved is a third necessity. Academic administrators vary greatly in the style of their operations, and for some administrators a need to maintain congenial relationships may seem to bar the way to expecting and getting efficient and exacting performance. But without the administrator's setting clear expectations, assisting others to come up to them, being firm about deadlines, and acting promptly and fairly in discharging supervisory responsibilities, the work of a department or college may go on neither congenially nor efficiently.

Expectations as to evaluation and accountability have risen in the last decade in all aspects of academic performance. Periodic review is certainly preferable to spasmodic attention to crises. Periodic review is a chance to clarify both what is being attempted and what progress is being made. Wise administrators do not so much pass judgment on others as involve and assist others in arriving at judgments useful to performing the task at hand. As with grading students' work, the object of evaluating the work of an individual or a group is to further that work and not merely to rank it.

"I spy on 'em to beat hell," one candid department chairman replied (Brann and Emmet, 1972, p. 12) in answer to a query about how he evaluated faculty teaching effectiveness. Good administrators are probably pretty good spies in many ways and good, too, at not being branded as spies. Experience alone may enable an administrator to develop a somewhat accurate sense of when performance of tasks is going well or poorly. Such a sense can be a useful supplement to more formal means of monitoring the work of others.

Axiom Six. *Learning to write and speak simple, serviceable English and to handle simple business machines can be powerful aids to getting things done.*

Simply to get things done, academic administrators must be capable users of language. The lamentations about students being unable to write are hardly defensible until department chairpersons, of English departments, too, and deans, of humanities as well as science, are capable of writing easily and well. If one must agonize over either routine spoken or written communication with a staff, there is almost a certainty that too little communicating will be going on. If every letter has to be labored into existence, it is certain correspondence will pile up, expected courtesies be passed over, and important matters be delayed or avoided for want of adequate expression.

As administrators rise up the academic ladder, the temptation to find someone else to serve as a speaking and writing voice becomes more and more attractive. At best, such a practice may be a way of putting specific talents to work. The gifted speechwriter finds employment; the harried president is freed for supposedly more demanding tasks. At worst, however, the administrator becomes a made-up personage, self-importance is magnified, and real substance diminished. Even the possibility of sorting out the routine communicating from the important and having someone else handle the routine is not as attractive as it might appear. It is not easy to find alter egos, and, even if it were, relying on someone else's abilities to speak and to write stands in the way of developing those very skills an administrator needs.

A curious paradox occurs within academic administration: A courting of certain kinds of business prerogatives—the placing of calls, the executive lunch—coexists with disdain for other business practices—a respect for office management and the use of business technology, for example. Persons engaged in intellectual work may pride themselves on lacking manual skills, on being unable to use simple tools or to master simple machines. No one expects a dean to repair the ailing office copier, but he or she should be able to

operate the common variety of office machines that facilitate communication. The flow of correspondence in and out of an academic
office makes it imperative that administrators develop business skills.
As it is useful for scholars to type, so it is useful for an administrator
to use a dictating machine. It is easier and cheaper, if less cozy, than
dictating to a secretary, and it takes care of routine correspondence
quickly. One acquires a technique adequate to meeting routine
correspondence, which, in most offices, does not raise expectations
of grace, wit, or eloquence. Saving time here permits one more time
to shape that written communication for which force and nuance
and precision of expression are vital.

Axiom Seven. *Developing a strong office staff begins with
dignifying the work that needs to be done.*

The comfortable assumption that there will always be a
willing clerical class (mostly female) to carry out the will of an
executive class (in academia, administrators and faculty, mostly
male) no longer can be made. Academic administrators may be
even more fond than other administrators of finding the perfect
secretary and turning much of the daily business over to her. In
some academic departments, fierce dragon ladies still guard inner
office, and the administrators they protect fondly refer to them as
"the real boss around here." But such academics are probably no
better than other administrators at conferring salaries and titles
that might justly reward the performance of these duties.

Nonacademic personnel—typists, secretaries, file clerks, research assistants, and the like—are customarily placed in distinctly
inferior positions to the professors whose work they facilitate. Too
often, they are at the disposal of a great number of people varying
widely in the care and respect they give to those who carry out
clerical tasks. They are often the first to be exposed to disgruntled
students, faculty, or members of the public. They develop loyalties
and animosities. They gossip, tell tales, spread rumors. They defend
those individuals they like and subvert those they dislike. Their
functioning well is too important to getting work done for a wise
administrator to neglect them. Whether these members of an administrative staff are temporary, part-time, or mere students, and
nonmajors at that, their ability to work with people, to have confidence in what they do, to commit themselves to whatever degree

their job warrants, to grow and take satisfaction in what they do—
these are as important as the specific skills they may possess.

The right connecting links between an academic administrator and the clerical staff are so crucial to an effectively functioning
operation that I will add an array of specific do's and don'ts:

* Do treat nonacademic personnel with respect. Much of getting
  things done depends on what they do.
* Do take care in choosing nonacademic personnel. Take some time
  to learn about the person, to locate some qualities of personal
  demeanor that may complement skills. Skill and efficiency are
  not incompatible with a pleasant manner.
* Do take advantage of the climate an educational institution offers
  to attract and hold superior personnel. Academic salaries may be
  lower than those in buisness, but the atmosphere for a person
  interested in learning is probably better.
* Do try to relate the aptitudes and interests of the person to those
  of the job.
* Do try to make individual jobs attractive, by offering more
  variety in any job than goes with being chained to a typewriter
  day by day or to a filing cabinet hour after hour.
* Do take advantage of the great number of bright students who
  need part-time work and who can learn many skills necessary to
  handling a flow of work.
* Do make the nonacademic personnel part of the enterprise rather
  than a separate group doing the low-level work.
* Don't leave the supervision and responsibility for office functioning altogether to someone else, or, if you do, make sure that person is directly and steadily responsible to you.
* Don't let contact with students or faculty come to take place pre-
  dominantly through the nonacademic staff.
* Don't let obvious deficiencies in the clerical operations of a
  department go unattended, uncorrected.
* Don't let able personnel be picked apart by conflicting demands
  and authorities.
* Don't harp upon bureaucratic inefficiencies of someone else's
  supporting staff—it will reflect back upon your respect for your
  own.

All of what I've written might gain the assent of administrators if they ever had time to read it. But, meanwhile, the daily
calendar is crowded, there are calls to be made and to be answered,
correspondence is coming in and must go out, appointments must
be met and made. Where is the time for the reading or reflecting
that might lighten the task? The answer is:

Axiom Eight. *There is never enough time. The able administrator
makes the available time fit.*

Part of that fitting is to find time each day for those things
to which deadlines are attached and on which the work of others
depends. These are periods in which the wise administrator does
disappear, maybe into an interior office, maybe to an office somewhere else, sometimes to return to the building after hours. How
one compensates for such time if it does come after hours is a matter
of personal management and satisfactions. At certain periods, administrative work is truly its own reward; that is, the tasks at hand
are such that seeing them well done rewards long, silent, after-hour
efforts. At other times, the luxury of being able to work uninter-
ruptedly may be reward in itself.

Such times should not be wasted on matters that can be
handled during office hours, when the regular business gets trans-
acted. A great many small, routine tasks can be taken care of in
those spaces that may appear between more preoccupying tasks.
That precious private time should be for more long-ranging
thoughts and for carrying out those goals greater than the discharging of daily responsibilities.

Drucker (1966) tells the story of an executive for whom he
acted as a consultant once a month for two years. His appointment
was always for an hour and a half with no more than one item on
the agenda. During those sessions, no telephones rang and no
secretaries interrupted. At the end of an hour and twenty minutes,
the executive would ask Drucker to sum up and outline the next
step. Drucker explains why the executive adopted this unvarying
routine: first, his attention span was about an hour and a half;
second, he felt even one important topic needed that much time;
and third, he knew that interruptions to this kind of focused thinking were deadly. Even with this careful kind of management,

Drucker estimates, half of this executive's working time was probably taken up by things of minor importance and dubious value.

Acknowledging the value of this insight from business administration, I think academic administrators are not always unwise in accepting a looser fit. An able academic administrator might well get used to working a good part of the day with the door open to the world. I think if offices were run with highest regard for the people they serve, the administrator would be out front receiving callers and the secretarial staff would be in the inner sanctum getting the work done. But as far as I know, such advice has only been followed once, when a new dean of a business school signaled his arrival by installing his desk in the hall, deliberately to find out first-hand from the flow of people what he needed to know and do.

On any administrator's desk should be a daily "To Do" list. There is wisdom in committing intentions and obligations to writing. Maintaining one's own "To Do" list becomes an inner and outer reminder, a goad if neglected too long, a source of satisfaction if items continue to get crossed off and others added. If any item stays on the list for weeks, the administrator should, in the interest both of sanity and efficiency, cross it off or put it on that other list: "Do Today!"

Somewhere close at hand should also be some form of "To Do" list that embraces longer prospects. Perhaps this should be more than a list, rather an accumulation of ideas, information, and reminders that must await fuller development before being ready for action. Most long-range plans depend on other people, and the administrator has some responsibility for moving others along. The best advice I ever gave as a consultant to higher education institutions was "Do Something!" This came after almost a day of meetings with various faculty and administration groups at a large university. For a year and a half, the groups had been trying to arrive at a plan of systematic faculty development. The faculty and administrators seemed to possess the necessary energy, good will, and intelligence to carry out any number of plans. But they were trapped amidst too many good ideas, with no one to decide which ones to adopt. "Trapped" may not be the right word, for most seemed to enjoy a certain felicity in inaction. Everyone's pet idea could be both entertained and fleshed out, every idea could enjoy hypothetical success, and no one had to be involved in the details of carrying out an actual program.

Clearly, someone needed to say, "Do something," even if that something turned out to be a firm "do nothing." Often, the administrator in charge will have to perform this function. Thus, as much a part of routine chores as keeping an appointment book is keeping tabs on the progress of long-range plans. Every administrator should hold himself to a yearly accounting in which he looks at all those things supposedly in progress, finds out where they are, sorts out those with some chance of success, and gets rid of those that are expendable.

I hope the dull, heavy, but regular throb of *efficiency* does not sound too monotonously through this chapter. There are tasks that are worth doing poorly, just as there are many things an administrator will inherit from a predecessor that are not worth doing at all. The progress of an administrator is likely to be from "Now I'll get all those things done that needed doing," to "Well, I won't be able to do all the things I wanted to do," to "Nothing can be done."

Axiom Nine. *You'll always fall behind; you'll never catch up.*

The last time I returned from leave, I exchanged pleasantries with a colleague who was nearing retirement after a long and illustrious career. Since I had been gone for half a year, I mentioned the difficulty I was experiencing in trying to get caught up. He looked at me benignly and said: "Six months behind? I'm three years behind and have no chance of catching up." I take heart in this license coming from one who had an undeniable record of scholarly achievements.

An administrator might well add to those actions subject to review how often he or she has been able to step completely away from the shop. If it has been very seldom or not at all, then one's calendar needs revising. Campuses furnish much attractive reflecting space, requiring nothing more from students or faculty or administrators than the time to make the most of it. Getting away for a long weekend may be no more salutary than walking across campus, particularly if that walk replaces business that can wait. Passing clouds have a way of putting human affairs into perspective; even damp rain and winter chill afford relief from indoor pondering. Administration requires such head clearing by the day, in eating lunch under a tree alone or talking to stray passersby; by the quarter, in spending afternoons in a library or a park or other sanctuary of one's choosing; by the year, in stepping back from the immediate doing to thinking about how it all might be fitting together.

Chapter 3

‑⫸‑⫸‑⫸‑⫸‑⫸‑⫸‑⫸‑⫸‑⫸

Simple Skills
for Simple Tasks

‑⫸

Though the mastery of simple skills does not comprise the whole art of administration, carrying out simple tasks well is one distinguishing mark of a good administrator. No amount of fitful brilliance can offset day-by-day bumbling. So here, near the beginning, is an ABC of some simple but inescapable administrative realities with some suggestions as to how they might be faced.

Advising. One should, if one can, give good advice. Most administrators will be asked for advice; often they will feel obliged to give it. Students have a right to see department heads; faculty will insist upon deans and chairpersons being accessible. Administrators at all levels should feel complimented when someone assumes, rightly or wrongly, that they have a store of advice useful to others.

Part of advising is routine, met by formalizing a student

advising staff and by maintaining office hours specifically set aside for students and faculty. Deans surveyed by Gould (1964, p. 33) described their office time as largely taken up by "a parade of people with problems moving in and out." More than time is involved, too; people seeking advice don't often do it by schedule. Many want it on the spot, and though a schedule of appointments may protect the administrator, it may not fully answer the needs of others.

Administrators who accept this reality will probably be generous in making themselves available. If time is to be saved, it will have to be done by handling individual appointments carefully. I can still remember how much of my time in chairing a department was taken up in letting people talk out problems they had already resolved or, more often, were not likely to resolve very soon. Occasionally, an advice giver may be the first one another person turns to; more often, he or she is somewhere in a line of persons from whom advice is being sought. Being sensitive to what lies behind a person's seeking advice and being patient are necessary to making a useful response; but firmness, sharpening and focusing of issues, shaping doubts and ponderings into questions, and posing or phrasing alternatives are necessary, too.

As one should have ways of bringing people to the point, so should one have ways of ending an advice-giving session. Long and formless conversations need to be channeled or brought to a halt. Sometimes the fault is with the other person; other times, it is with ourselves. At still other times, both parties are at fault, perhaps because no one finds the right words or gestures—no one wanting to appear discourteous or graceless or seeming to be pressed with more important matters—to bring it to an end. Few people seeking advice want it under a time clock, but few, too, benefit from conversations prolonged simply because neither party finds a way to break off.

Anticipating. Anticipating should be as much an administrative habit as returning calls promptly. It should be done systematically—and optimistically, if possible. Yes, faculty members will reach retirement age, graduate assistants will need attention, committees will turn in reports or have to be prodded into doing so, achievements will need to be recognized. Not everything can be anticipated, nor is there much health in anticipating disasters. Looking forward with pleasure helps counteract those times when one can only look forward with dread.

Authorizing. An administrator wishing to save time will do a great deal of authorizing. But the blanket act of assigning all routine business to someone else is unwise. Signing papers, for example, does not take all that much time, and it can be time well spent in keeping conversant with the nature and volume of routine business. Assigning all routine authorizations of apparently simple matters to a clerical staff—changes of registration or approval of student programs, for example—can lead to the tiresome joke that the secretaries run the department. Secretaries might more appreciate the humor if they were paid an administrator's wage. And administrators might more recognize the importance of their role in handling routine matters if they were to put themselves in a secretary's place and try to run that part of the operation.

Administrators must make clear to themselves and to the staff under them, as well as to the public served, where authority for important matters resides. Developing responsibility in a staff entails giving others authority over important matters as well as over routine ones. That should not mean that the authorizing administrator cannot act in the absence of the person to whom authority has been delegated or even contrary to that person's decision, preferably after gaining his or her concurrence. Where important responsibilities are vested in an administrator, authority must come to rest there. Claiming that the responsibility has been wholly turned over to someone else is usually only an irritating way of passing the buck.

Budgeting. Working with the budget severely tests an administrator, for the budget is full of vexing details and yet bears importantly upon everything else. Inevitably, the budget arouses strong personal feelings. It cannot be long put off nor delegated entirely to others. At most, a chairperson or dean may have an executive or budget committee to share responsibilities and to relieve some pressures from individuals seeking favorable financial treatment for themselves or for the programs and interests they support.

The budget reminds an administrator that there are limits to what a department or college can do, limits to what an administrator can accomplish or even attempt, and limits to what a faculty can reasonably expect. Within those limits, budget making is constantly a matter of making choices. Budgeting one's time, conserving faculty energies, eliminating waste in academic programs, shifting attention from one aspect of a curriculum to another—all these are budgetary in nature. The budget can be an awful fact of administrative life, the bookkeeping chore that clouds one's vision. Still, even such a visionary as Thoreau began *Walden* with a chapter on "Economy." "I have always endeavored to acquire strict business habits," he writes; "they are indispensable to every man" (1957, p. 13).

Calling meetings. Though meetings typically occupy much of an administrator's time, few develop real skill in *calling* meetings. The basic considerations are simple: (1) not holding too many or too few, (2) finding a time convenient as well as acceptable to most participants, and (3) preparing sufficiently in advance.

Let me comment briefly and simply on each of these. No group ever agrees upon the exact number of meetings that best serves the business needing to be done, the desires of individuals to have a say in that business, and the convenience of all those involved. Nevertheless, thoughtfully considering with the group when and how often to meet is better than being arbitrary about it. Moreover, since preferences and conditions change, periodic reconsideration of these questions has to be given.

Meetings fall into these categories: general business meetings scheduled at regularly specified times; meetings necessary to conducting specific business, such as appointments, promotions, consideration of committee reports, and the like; meetings arising out of unanticipated problems or crises; and meetings that address large questions of policy or direction. In most departments, a large number of meetings seems unavoidable, and finding a time when everyone can get together is no small problem. A chairperson is well advised to arrange class schedules so that there are some hours in which all faculty are free. (It might be an equally good idea to see that students' schedules also made provisions for common gathering times.) In addition, those who call meetings should be sensitive to obviously bad times for meetings—the first and last weeks of a term, for example, or periods when exams are being read and grades assigned. Conflicts with other meetings or with events on campus should also be identified and avoided. An awareness of customary patterns of work may eliminate meeting times that infringe upon faculty's time for study or other commitments. Noon luncheons may be all right if the group is small and convivial, but they are poor occasions for any business that involves strenuous discussion and decision making. They also slight the importance of lunch, the midday break, which should honor *idle-* more than *busy*-ness.

Though the regularly scheduled department meeting is a fixture of academic life, I think its advisability should be questioned. There are enough meetings that *have* to be held to satisfy faculty members, and regular meetings often lack the focus and planning that go with facing specific problems and issues. Faculty members, of course, can be brought together profitably for other reasons than to face problems and issues, but such gatherings might wisely be kept apart from the conventional department meeting. Few meetings should be called without at least a week's notice. An administrative calendar, published at the beginning of the term, can usefully inform everyone of anticipated times of necessary meetings without establishing a pattern of regular meetings every week or month.

The chief purpose of most meetings should be face-to-face exchange of informed opinion, and that purpose should guide advance preparation. Gathering of facts, written statements of proposals and ideas, identification of issues should all be a part of advance planning. Any meetings—and universities have hundreds of them—that are to reach decisions on the basis of information available before the meeting should not proceed without a fair assurance that most members of the deciding group have become acquainted with and even thought about the issues. Careful preparation for meetings increases the possibility that most of the participants will be involved and that most of the time will be spent at the center of issues.

Administrators are often assisted in the planning of meetings by steering committees, executive committees, policy committees— useful and familiar means of shaping and defining agendas. Such committees should not be mere tools of an administrator nor bypassed in practice. Neither should they be the only means by which an individual faculty member can raise an issue or assure its formal consideration. Prince (1970, p. 11) voices the committee member's chronic complaints. "Our meetings are boring. My ideas are seldom heard. Often we don't come to grips with the real problem." Such complaints may arise because many members of the group feel they have no stake in the meeting, no voice in why it's being called, and only a hazy idea of the issues to be faced. Increasing opportunities for participants to have a hand in shaping the agenda and defining issues before meetings may be the first step toward making meetings themselves profitable.

Conducting Meetings. Being able to conduct a good meeting is a developable skill. Its components are (1) making clear what is to be attempted and within what time, (2) conducting matters with dispatch, without appearing to rush them through, (3) being fair, (4) accomplishing intentions, and (5) adjourning at a reasonable time. Prince (1970, p. 31) writes: "Nearly all chairmen we have observed in our research use a casual, personal fusion of *Robert's Rules*, legal, military, and Dale Carnegie models." He finds that these models, however, do not foster leadership behavior that he deems highly desirable: not competing with participants, listening intently, keeping the energy level high, avoiding manipulation, reducing defensiveness among participants, drawing upon all participants, and clarifying and fostering understanding. Drawing upon research into the dynamics of groups, Prince advocates a meeting model in which "the leader's whole attention is devoted to helping the group use its wits" (p. 6).

Emphasizing the cooperative and collective achievements that may come out of successful meetings does not diminish the responsibilities of the leader. Following parliamentary procedures, even with some strictness, need not result in a stiff, legalistic atmosphere. Individuals vary greatly in their use of such procedures and in their resistance to them. The one who conducts meetings by these rules needs to know them thoroughly and to educate others in their use. Getting individuals to make motions instead of speeches, to discuss motions rather than air prejudices, to sense the harm and good in tabling and calling the question and amending are responsibilities a chairperson can help develop in a faculty. In addition, there are skills those who preside over meetings must develop in themselves: clarifying motions and seeing that they are understood by all; keeping track of those wanting to be recognized and being fair in giving recognition; holding individuals to the question but not stifling discussion; sensing when debate has moved to a consensus or has reached a division that further discussion is not likely to resolve; keeping the group aware of time but not oppressed by it; and intervening to sharpen issues, to clarify, to abbreviate debate, to move to another item on the agenda. Likert (1967, p. 57), in attempting to define the character of effective sales organizations, reached the conclusion that "group meetings are effective when the manager (or supervisor) does a competent job of presiding over the interactions among the men." That could well be an academic administrator's goal in making the most of the dynamics of meetings. To state this goal in more specific terms of my own, I think a chairperson must see to moving things along without driving them, to leading people rather than manipulating them, and to being fair and impartial but not relinquishing the leadership role.

Ultimately, chairpersons succeed as conductors of meetings by the measure of what meetings accomplish. If faculty members come out of a two-hour meeting with a general feeling that fifteen minutes' worth of work has been done, all the efforts of the chair to be impartial, fair, considerate, and wise will have been for naught. Conversely, if tough decisions are reached within a reasonable amount of time, the chair will be excused for exercising tighter control than all parties might like. If, amidst contentious individuals, prickly issues, and actions that affect even one person adversely, a chair can maintain humor, perspective, and sympathy, larger goals than reaching decisions will have been achieved. If most meetings are adjourned within that period of time when participants begin to feel they've had enough, the chairperson will be regarded as miraculous indeed.

Defending. Argyris (1957, pp. 41–47) has a concise list of defense mechanisms with which individuals resist threats to the self without changing their own behaviors. Changing behavior often requires admitting that one is wrong or that there is a more desirable way to behave than the customary and comfortable one.

Defending oneself and one's actions may be regarded by some as a necessary part of administration rather than as a largely destructive aspect of human personality. Anger, aggression, guilt, denial, inhibition, overcompensation, suppression, projection, ambivalence, and vacillation, as administrative behaviors, are wasters of precious psychic energy both of administrators and the people they may be defending themselves against.

Discussing. Discussing is not talking, or telling, or even listening. It is a process of exchange, in which getting others to express their views is as important as expressing one's own.

Enlisting. Beyond encouraging individuals, which is basic to getting the most out of them, is the active enlisting of individuals to work at specific tasks. It is different from appointing, or electing, or getting elected. It may not even be connected with a specific task. But it is a skill administrators should be constantly sharpening and practicing in diverse ways. Enlisting students in learning, faculty in teaching, human beings in fulfilling their aims and assisting in the aims of others draws upon an administrator's highest powers. And yet, successful efforts to enlist individuals in the learning enterprise may be as simple as recognizing that a certain faculty member has seldom been asked to do anything and might be extraordinarily responsive to the right invitation.

Expediting. As enlisting goes beyond encouraging, so does expediting go beyond getting things done. Expediting is aimed at seeing that others get things done, things that serve not only the administrator's good or the other person's good but the common good. An ideal administrator should spend more time in helping others around, through, and over bureaucratic obstacles than in defending such obstacles or piling up more.

Forgetting. Everyone forgets. The absent-minded professor is legendary. The administrator has less of a margin for being forgetful, or being forgiven for forgetting, or being forgiving when others forget. The appointment calendar, the secretary, the pocket reminder, and the alarm clock wristwatch are some ordinary aids to memory. But more important is an inner clock, which is not so much chronological as occasional. Its conjunction of parts rings bells that bring to mind larger aims too often forgotten despite daily reminders. If this clock is faithful to its erratic functionings, it will not let important matters be completely forgotten. It will ring at awkward hours, reminding its possessor that obligations have not been met, people have not been informed, proposals not addressed, letters not sent. Sometimes, working well, it may tick fitfully and stop altogether, proving an aid to the necessary forgetting of the angers and disappointments of a given day.

Gathering. In my part of the country, the Mormons are still animated by the idea of *gathering*. Theologically, I think, it refers to the ultimate gathering, the reuniting of all good souls in Heaven. In this world, it defines the strong impulse of those who have left Zion, the temporal world of which Salt Lake City is the center, to return there. In the personal life of the believers, it is one of the forces responsible for the intensely social character of Mormon life and the sense of community that flourishes among the faithful.

In academic life, *gathering* is a term preferable to *summoning* or *communing* or even *partying*. Though the latter is a commonplace of academic life, its true importance is rarely recognized. Administrators must accept responsibility for and develop skill in bringing people together, actually as well as metaphorically. Helping others to share pleasures and griefs is a true act of "ministering"; besides, the department office has the means of sending out the invitations. A chairperson could do worse than become master of revels.

Honoring. As with gathering, so with honoring. Though academic life carries from its past much ceremonial and traditional honoring, the present has eroded much of that away. Even were it not part of an institution's traditions, the honoring of people and activities is a necessary part of an administrator's skills. I am not talking about awarding false honors, pumping up egos that as often as not need deflating. I am talking about honoring the unheralded services that are an intrinsic part of scholarship and teaching, and the manifestations of learning that go unmarked. So, outside of the elections to honorary societies, the gold watch at retirement, the festschrift in the sunset years, there are numerous opportunities for honoring.

Identifying. An administrator should also be an *identifier*, a *namer*. More precisely, it is often the administrator's exercise of insight and inquiry that identifies the source of a problem or that identifies those many and subtle factors that have created a problem. So, too, must administrators identify opportunities, directions to take, and projects to be undertaken. More difficult to identify is the temper of a group or of key individuals in a group who must be reckoned with in achieving consensus or cooperation. Always vital, of course, is identifying the right person for the right job, the right action to motivate the right person, the right choice of one's own actions in relation to another's.

Initiating. The power to initiate is a formidable parliamentary power. At one time, in collegiate administration, administrators seemed to be clearly conceded this power. A more recent administrative stance makes less of this power and assumes that the faculty will do the initiating and the administration will carry out what has been proposed. While the older structure clearly defined administrative and faculty roles, the new one supposes that individual faculty members or groups of faculty will be prolific in initiating ideas and proposals. The result may be an administration somewhat disappointed in the faculty's ability to think of things for them to do and a faculty wondering what it is that administrators are doing.

Justifying. At times, hard-pressed administrators may find themselves spending too much time justifying their activities. In ordinary times, faculty activities are presumed to be self-justifying; departments rely heavily on self-justification. Lately, the justification for higher education, itself, has become a public question. The best justification for a department's and its faculty's activities is the learning they foster. The administrator's function is to give those accomplishments visibility before the public.

Knowing. Administrators are expected to know more about some things than faculty. Since few of these subjects are concerns of academic disciplines, the new administrator may find it hard to exercise scholarly habits of mind over such matters as grade inflation, the quality of duplicating equipment, or what has been happening to enrollments. Knowledge about such subjects, however, abounds and can be discovered, assessed, and applied just as surely as can knowledge within a discipline. Administrators have the responsibility of exposing themselves to the search tools, periodicals, books, and oral exchange, which can raise the level of knowing in routine as well as important matters. Faculties expect their administrators to be informed, to keep records, to conduct studies, to keep up with what is happening outside the department or college, and to translate different kinds of information into forms that assist the faculty in making wise decisions. It is one thing to be a dumb administrator; it is another to be smart but not to know much.

Listening. Listening is one of those human capabilities that has become a part of the academic curriculum. Reading, writing, and arithmetic no longer suffice as basics; listening, articulating, and computing more nearly bring the young up to date. Whether or not students can learn to listen through formal instruction, I think administrators can do so only with great difficulty. Transforming a compulsive talker into a halfway good listener is as difficult as effecting any other consequential change in personality. The ordinarily articulate faculty member may find that the listening and lying back that fall to an administrator provide a psychological relief from talking. Thus, an ability to listen may develop from modifying one's habits in response to what new situations seem to call for.

Meddling and Monitoring. In playing a part in others' actions within an organization, an administrator can either frustrate or further the organization's purposes. Some persons need only to be left alone; others to be watched; and still others to be set in motion and helped along. The distance between meddling and monitoring is very small. Taking an interest in another's work, letting that interest lead to suggestions, and worrying about results easily slide over into meddling. Even doing the necessary monitoring that goes with seeing that a job gets done may be regarded as meddling. And, in truth, too great a concern for how a person is doing a job may detract from the performance the supervisor is trying to encourage. The trick is to be able to show an interest in another person's work and even to evaluate that work without interfering with the successful aspects of performance.

Neglecting. "Benign neglect" had its brief hour as a phrase, just long enough for us to recognize that rhetoric is never adequate to dealing with social problems. Neglect is not to be confused with letting things alone. Neglect is baneful, implying a willful refusal to give attention to that which is worthy or needful of attention. Letting things alone implies a restraint growing out of understanding and trust. Behind neglect is at best an inadvertent failure to care, at worst a deliberate decision not to care. Administrators who neglect things either attach no great importance to them or, taking a negative stance toward them, hope they will go away. There are many matters that are well left alone, few that profit from neglect.

Opposing. The art of opposing embraces carefully studied and applied techniques as well as spontaneous wellings up of personality and character. A loyal opposition may incline toward the former, Melville's saying "No! in thunder" toward the latter. Administrative work gives the person doing it many opportunities to become expert at opposing. An opposition that still leaves room for opposed energies to find other directions may be the highest development of this expertise. All the resources of personality enter into successful opposing: humor, compassion, understanding, sympathy, and some resources of a less-accepted kind: anger, indignation, adamancy, outrage. A firm and respected character may be the indispensable basis for successful opposition. In crises, one must be able to draw upon one's reputation for reasonableness and integrity, the more important as a situation may provoke charges of self-righteousness, self-interest, and bullheadedness.

Pleasing, Pacifying, and Placating. All these are necessary to getting along with others, though all have unpleasant connotations. We don't ordinarily want to please someone just for that reason, and we feel worse if we *have* to please someone. Yet being pleasant, giving pleasure, pleasing others, is not shunned except by misanthropes. And blessed are the peacemakers, regardless of how impatient administrators get with having to pacify and placate members of their staff.

Questioning. Administrators should probably ask more questions than they do. How else can they find out about the strengths and weaknesses of instruction, the changing interests of students, the satisfactions and discontents of the faculty, the standing of a department or college within the university? And what kind of shrewder questioning must go on to identify the reality beneath appearances? If new administrators established at the outset that they needed to find out about many things and that asking simple and direct questions was their way of finding out, they might more quickly gain the understanding and respect of the faculty. Some administrators may not ask questions until too late, when things have gone so far wrong that questions are met only with defensiveness, resentment, blame, and covering up.

Rationalizing. In the face of all the problems that administrators must cope with, all the expectations made of them, and all the forces even a skillful administrator cannot control, stoicism may be an attractive philosophy to embrace and rationalizing a characteristic gesture. If one's individual performance falters, well, the whole administrative structure is a little infirm, anyway. If the faculty is insecure, insecurity may make them work harder. If the students complain, that's the nature of students. If the curriculum is in chaos, that's the nature of curriculums. If messages don't get through, that's the nature of bureaucracy. And if one's administrative performance leaves one exhausted but unfulfilled, full of grief and short on accomplishments, that is not only the nature of administration but the hard lot that must be borne. Tempting as these stoical postures may be, a more positive stance better suits administrators and those they serve. Effective performance and the accomplishments that go with it make rationalizing unnecessary, except perhaps wisely to reflect that one's own efforts are seldom wholly responsible for one's success.

Scheduling. Scheduling is an irritation to many administrators and a job often assigned to someone else. It often appears to be purely clerical work: putting dates and hours on a chart and filling in the blanks. It can stand for that large amount of administrative work within higher education that seems inseparable from and is yet remote from teaching and learning. Like advising, scheduling is not something that an administrator can totally give over to someone else. For scheduling is connected not merely to rooms and numbers but to human preferences and aversions. Scheduling is one way an administrator has of staying in touch with the faculty and curriculum. Though scheduling can be done mechanically, those involved in doing it need to know students, faculty, and subject matter. Like other seemingly mechanical functions, it should not be regarded as being beneath the administrator's attention.

Teaching. Administrators do not have to give up teaching, even though they may not appear regularly in the classroom. Successful administration requires a great deal of teaching of one's colleagues, often without their being made aware of it. A department faculty may be likened to a class; while meetings may give the administrator a chance to shine, what the class achieves depends on far more than meetings. There are texts and assignments and evaluation responsibilities, too, and far less authority to call on to exact performance from faculty than the teacher has to get work out of students. In the end, good administering, like good teaching, makes the most of the interacting relationships through which everyone learns.

Understanding. The search for understanding of oneself, of the people with whom one works, of the system, of the small and large aims of people and system—how much of an administrator's time goes into that search! To feel understood is a strong human desire. Faculty members expect to be understood by administrators, even though they may extend little enough understanding in turn. The most difficult to deal with are those often misunderstood individuals whose trouble begins with not understanding themselves. *"We cannot understand ourselves unless we understand others,"* Argyris (1957, p. 48) writes, *"and we cannot understand others unless we understand ourselves."*

Voting. Voting is a necessary part of group decision making, though some departments may rely upon nonvoting consensus and others upon administrators' decisions. In the important matters of appointment, promotion, and tenure, voting is usually defined by institutional statutes. In other important matters, voting may be defined by departmental regulations or by custom as the way of finally reaching decisions. Parliamentary procedures define the processes by which a group arrives at a vote and a vote is finally taken. An administrator is like any civic-minded person, but with even more responsibility for getting out the vote, seeing that a vote is not coerced or corrupted, and abiding by the resulting decision.

Waiting. Patience is an ordinary virtue that needs little adapting to fit an administrator's needs. In my own administrative experience, the hardest kind of waiting was that which was necessary to complete any task that required the participation of many people. I had to learn to wait for calls to be returned, for other administrators to get back to campus, for funds to become available. I had to wait and hope for many kinds of changes. Through all the waiting, I had also to find ways of working amidst a good many loose ends. Somehow I managed to temper personal impatience with greater regard for the slower processess by which groups work.

And yet, that is not the whole story, for there are such things as inexcusable delays and lethargy disguised as deliberation, for which impatience deserves to be the response.

Yielding. Winning some and losing some are the homeliest facts of administrative striving. Yielding gracefully is part of losing. Further, an administrator's responsibility is to keep divisions from paralyzing action. That responsibility entails an anticipation of an evenly split vote and skillful intervention to head off polarization of an issue. Testing sentiment and suggesting accommodations are two common devices an administrator can use. The toughness to force votes or to resist pressures to bring a question to a vote may also be demanded of an administrator.

Yielding should not be waffling, a token kind of resistance to one faction or another with an ultimate giving in or equivocating. Yielding in one particular may enable an administrator to stand firm on a more important one. An administrator's yielding to the department's will is not a matter of accepting defeat but of recognizing that it is the department that an administrator serves. Faculties accept administrative leadership and even authority, but they ultimately defeat any administrator who insists on always having his way.

Once a decision is reached, no delaying actions should accompany the administrator's carrying out a course of action he may not personally favor. If the decision is close, following through effectively will probably require efforts to win over the opposition. Administrators who appear to yield in the face of overwhelming opposition and then undermine the majority decision by slow or contrary implementation are only likely to succeed in the short run and lose both their authority and position in the long run.

X and Z. As this purports to be an ABC of some relatively simple administrative responsibilities, X and Z can stand for everything that has been left out. This might include *xenophobia*, the tendency to overreact to almost anything foreign to one's own experience, or *x ray*, as in x-ray vision, which, like being able to jump over a budget at a single bound, is a useful power to have. And it might end with *zigzag*, the way successful administrators may have to move to get from A to Z.

Chapter 4

>>>->>>->>>->>>->>>->>>->>>->>>->>>

Communicating

>>>->>>->>>->>>->>>->>>->>>->>>->>>->>>->>>->>>->>>->>>->>>->>>->>>

Many college administrators are afraid of communication: Most talk about the necessity for it; few communicate well. I think this generalization applies as much to chairpersons of departments of English or speech or even communications as to those in less verbalizing disciplines. Within the university at large, communication tends to be bureaucratic, fitful, and seldom concerned directly with teaching and learning. Not too many years past, I kept track of the written communications from an academic vice-president to the faculty. Aside from an invitation to attend the opening-of-the-year ceremonies, three messages communicated the sum of that administrator's inspiration: Contribute to the United Fund, turn out the lights, and don't smoke in the classroom.

Likert (1967), studying communication in business organizations, found the communication process of the most productive organizations to be characterized by the following: much interaction with both individuals and groups; a flow of information

41

down, up, and among peers; general acceptance of communication from above and accurate flow of communication from below; and generally open and candid questioning. Such communication is part of an atmosphere that fosters trusting and productive interaction throughout the organization.

The literature of college and university administration similarly emphasizes the necessity for a climate in which communication can flourish. Openness in administration is necessary to establishing that climate. Doors and minds and channels of communication must be open. Access to people, to information, to resources must be open. Privilege and status, protocol and lines of authority, keep people from being open. Democracy in the administering of our colleges and universities is no troublesome privilege being periodically clamored for by some students and faculty; it is intrinsic to the open conduct of our main business: the free flow and exchange of ideas. The Carnegie Commission's (1973a, pp. 197–200) recommendations on governance of higher education denotes four pages in an appendix to "Openness of Decision Making and Communications," emphasizing that "To communicate effectively administrators must be open and candid in giving reasons for decisions and actions."

Deans, chairpersons, directors, and vice-presidents—all are responsible for a systematic gathering and making use of relevant information. A large part of that information concerns the internal operations of the college or department or unit. Another part concerns information from the outside that might usefully inform internal operations. Few administrators can do this job by themselves. Other matters have and deserve priority. But that fact only increases the necessity for seeing (1) that the gathering of information is done and done well, (2) that the information gets examined and pondered, and (3) that it gets disseminated effectively. Administrators cannot escape being involved in these processes; the fortunate ones will be those who establish ways in which all these things are done well.

Universities probably pay too little serious attention to the increase of information and the consequences for those who work with it or are affected by it. Any large collegial unit would find money and time well spent that was directed toward gathering and screening information and seeing that people who needed to be informed were informed. I have called attention elsewhere (Eble, 1972, pp. 181–182) to the establishing of a university "information office" solely concerned with scanning the vast amount of information coming into a university and channeling it into the hands of those who need it. Within the humanities, whose practitioners are trained in gathering written information, in analyzing and writing, and in developing rhetorical skills, there is surely room for a job category of *information specialist.* Some of the research Ph.D. candidates now might do better to turn to examining how information within an institution might be put to use.

A person professionally employed as an information specialist for a college or department should have training in psychology or an experientially acquired understanding of why individuals and groups behave as they do. For the problem in communicating is not only that information is not gathered and messages are not sent out but that messages are not received and acted upon. There are dozens of reasons for failures to communicate, some residing in conditions outside the receiving apparatus of the individual and some attributable to the inner workings of that apparatus. Ready access to information may be regarded by some academics as being able to find out whatever it is one wishes to find out without making much effort. Such a view is unrealistic, but too little help is available to assist faculty members in sorting and filing and selecting from the ceaseless flow of messages coming in. For it should be remembered that the faculty members are assailed not just by internal communications affecting the educational operation but by an ever-increasing flood of words, oral and written, bearing upon their scholarly work.

As to the psychological receptivity of those who would be communicated with, *reinforcement, set* and *interference* are as important to that receptivity as they are to learning. Messages are not likely to be received unless there is reinforcement for those who respond to them. The *set* of the receiver—biases for or against the sender of the message or the form in which it comes—explains both success and failure in communicating. Resistances are established on campus to almost every form of communication: statistics, printouts, bar graphs, visuals, and words themselves. Even when rein-

forcement is forthcoming and predispositions favorable, communication of any one kind has to overcome the interference set up by
competing messages.

Amidst all those reasons human beings may have for resisting as well as responding to an administrator's efforts to communicate, the administrator may give up trying or settle for an amiable
ineffectuality. My own views about communicating come not only
from observing many different colleges and universities and departments but also from being in a discipline—English—in which communication is a professional concern. I am still surprised that an
average English department, which so prides itself on dealing with
the written word and which presumes to teach writing and reading,
communicates so poorly in writing within its own province. Like all
other departments, most English departments adopt one gray tone
for summoning to meetings, raising policy questions, passing on
information, and the like. The prose is at best serviceable; piling
up on one's desk, it can become depressing. The occasional message
that has something of wit or geniality—style of any kind—is rare.
Here is a sampling of what accumulates over a year—typical, I
think, of both substance and manner of expression:

> The department has been informed that salary
> increments for next year will not be increased except as
> they can be substantiated by evidence of merit. Could you
> submit a page or two on which you list publications,
> papers read, editing, committee service (departmental,
> university, community, national), and any other per-
> tinent details?

> Please check your classrooms for the spring
> quarter so that we can try to make any changes you con-
> sider necessary or desirable.

> Dean _____ needs a list of facutly members in-
> volved in research projects (funded or unfunded by out-
> side or interior sources) and a brief description affording
> salient details of and progress on the project. Will those
> of you to whom this applies please reply with promptness.

> Our perennial problem of secretarial workload has
> surfaced again. I think we would all agree that the de-

partment is committed to providing full and effective secretarial support for the faculty. While all of us have needs that arise suddenly and should be accommodated, the system breaks down when we have too many rush jobs at the same time.

The stipend schedule for TAs and TFs which will appertain next year has been newly constituted. Class visitation fills a need to give TAs and TFs notice that the department exercises a supervisory and tutelary responsibility over graduate student teaching. The new information sheets offer a convenient codification of policies that have been in effect for some time.

Input on the new coffee system is welcome.

These are random samples drawn from my own department's memos. For all its brevity, the last may be the worst. What chemistry of the mind turns *coffee* into a *system* and makes it susceptible to *input?* The style matches the substance in these not just uninspiring but dispiriting messages.

The jargon of specialized academic disciplines makes communicating across the university even more difficult than within a department. The language used in the study of communication and organizational behavior is often, in itself, a barrier to communication. "An organization," I learn from a scholarly book in this field, "is an open, dynamic, multi-goal-seeking, purposeful system that has elements of concreteness or abstraction." And, seeking further, I find that "one advantage of a system's philosophy is that its holistic character allows one to analyze the effects of change on total system performance and output generation and to analyze subsystem behavior as it interfaces with the broader system."

I cite these examples only as a plea for simple, direct, and—yes—personal address in spoken and written communication. The spoken word from an administrator to a faculty member or a faculty member to a student has its own built-in corrective. Bewilderment or confusion has a way of registering on a person's face. Anger and incredulity and outrage show themselves even more plainly. Few administrators witness responses to written messages. And many, anticipating the worst and mindful of just the kind of criticism I have just made here about writing, may give up trying for an effective tone and substance. Unfortunately, though too much written communication may be a characteristic of bureaucratic and academic institutions, a great deal of written communication for both routine and nonroutine matters is inescapable.

Let me comment briefly on the necessity for putting things into writing. One of the first, and I think best, lessons I learned as an administrator was to write almost everything down. I learned it the hard way, out of disagreements with faculty members over things they said I had said and I said I had not said. All important matters of agreement between one person and another deserve to be put in writing on the spot. In the long run, it saves time and tempers. I also found written reminders absolutely necessary to keep me from forgetting things, many of them small in consequence to me but not to someone else. A large part of my time was spent in writing memos and notices, the necessary informing of others that constitutes so much administrative communication.

With the multiplication of copiers and duplicators, the blizzard of written notices has certainly increased. A faculty member may long to get some first-class mail but will have no shortage of no-class messages. Are there ways to decrease the bulk and increase the impact of verbal messages? One commonly adopted way is to restrict what can be put into the mail. Mailing bureaus at large universities can be ordered to accept only approved notices for general free circulation. Such moves, like citizens' drives to eliminate junk mail, achieve little success. Another way is to develop weekly calendars of events. These reduce the number of individual announcements and help faculty members plan their time but do not serve for every kind of information. A third way is to use other means of conveying certain kinds of information: a bulletin board for routine announcements, the telephone to summon small groups for important meetings, personal contact. None of these will reach everyone or obviate the need for written communication. The question behind a plethora of written notices is whether the purposes that occasion the notices and summonings are all justified. Put simply, too many announcements may mean too much going on and too little sorting out of the important from the unimportant. There is not a campus in the country that would not be served by

administrators willing to take a stand against the busy-ness that so
clogs communication lines and so thwarts efforts to establish
community.

The question an administrator should ask is not primarily,
"Should I put this notice in the box?" but "Is this meeting necessary?" One way of cutting down on meetings and the number of
notices that announce them is to make writing count for more in
carrying on dialogue within an academic group. Written discussion
of issues has the great advantage of permitting the writer to set
forth without interruption the main lines of argument, the pros and
cons, the background information necessary for discussion. For the
reader, it has the advantage of being available for perusal on one's
own time and in relation to other relevant materials that may be at
hand or that can be looked up. If such communication is to be
effective, a forceful and persuasive writer should be at one end, a
receptive reader at the other.

The two probably go together. And breaking out of the
expected administrative prose may be the beginning of dialogue,
even before any face-to-face meeting. There are risks, certainly.
Even the simplest of announcements can be misunderstood. Merely
multiplying the number of words increases the possibilities. If written communication is confined to the mere conveying of necessary
information, that very sameness reduces the effectiveness of the
messages themselves. Worse, it may create an impression that faculty engaged in the genuine excitement of teaching and learning
are, in fact, concerned chiefly with scheduling, attending meetings,
ordering books, arranging classes, screening personnel, weighing
promotions, contributing to causes, checking serial numbers, accounting for supplies, locking doors, replacing erasers, and the like.
Granting the necessity of written messages and yet attempting to
reduce their number, a good administrator must concentrate on
conveying important information in effective ways.

The necessary business of running a college or department
will continue to provide the stuff for a very basic kind of writing.
But if administrators are to generate more consequential writing
from themselves or from their staffs, they must find time to think
freely and imaginatively and turn their thinking and reading and
experiencing into words that will stimulate others to articulate their

views. To some degree, all college and university administrators must be able speakers and writers. But how rare is a president who openly avows, as did the late Richard Bailey of Hamline University, that "administrators should be seen and heard." Bailey practiced his belief unashamedly, writing a column that appeared frequently in the *Minneapolis Star:* "I happen to think that a great many college presidents could, and should, be writing editorial columns for maximum visibility for themselves and for the institutions they head" (Mauer, 1976, p. 206). At the least, deans and chairpersons and the higher officers of the university, whatever their personal talents, should be capable of drawing on other talents to raise internal college and university communication above the merely informing level.

The higher purpose of communication within a social structure, McGregor (1967, p. 27) affirms, is to respond to human needs. He quotes Hamburg (in Knapp, 1963, p. 312): "Each person craves response from his human environment. It may be viewed as a hunger, not unlike that for food, but more generalized. Under varying conditions it may be expressed as a desire for contact, for recognition and acceptance, for approval, for esteem." It is this nagging kind of need that is met by keeping communication flowing both ways and in various engaging ways. This is not to belittle information, rather to plead for an enhancing of information by developing the skills through which it is conveyed and exchanged. Administrators commonly have a wider view of higher education than faculty because they expose themselves to more information about a wider range of subjects and face a wider variety of demands and expectations. Indeed, one of the major functions of administrators is to lessen the provincialism of a faculty, to act both as conduits for information and sources of stimulation.

Every administrator should have or develop some special means of answering a group's need for *communing* as distinguished from *communicating.* It might constitute a series of small gatherings designed to reach all members of a staff over a period of time, or invitations to lunch, or deliberately initiated conversations. Its written form might be that of a newsletter, a necessity in a large department and an opportunity to get beyond the stuff of memos and notices and reminders. Freed from a regular format or schedule, such a publication is the place to entertain ideas, confront and define issues, invite exchange, and tap a department's collective imagination and wit as much as its thought.

Lively and productive interplay between written and spoken communication is a goal worth striving for. Management analysts deplore the dominance of one-way communication and urge executives to establish the kind of climate and conditions that foster interaction and exchange. What administrators do to improve communication in specific ways is no more important than the many daily acts through which they relate to others. A note about the use of the telephone will serve to call attention to this dimension of daily communicating.

Faculty sensitivities are easily aroused by any obstruction to personal communication with an administrator. Playing status and authority games, with or without the aid of the telephone, is not worth an administrator's time. Placing calls oneself is worth the little time it may take in light of the good will fostered by not forcing the person being called to wait for an eminence to come on the line. Returning calls promptly is another simple sign of respect. If it is not routinely possible to do so, setting aside times at the beginning and end of the day will serve the same purpose. It will also give others the sense of being able to get through. More face-to-face talking may be better than depending too much on the phone. One of the best chairmen I have known hardly ever talked to a faculty member by phone, and probably never on his own initiative. Most often his talks were in the faculty member's office. A walk down the hall or to another building is good for one's health as well as very good for the relations between an administrator and his or her colleagues.

Effective communication is never easy. But verbalizing ideas and plans and objectives is as necessary to fulfilling an organization's aims as bringing people together. Drucker (1970, p. 3), noting the rising interest in communications in management during the past fifty years, observes, "The noise level has gone up so fast that no one can really listen to all that babble about communication. But there is clearly less and less communicating." And yet, Drucker, like many others concerned with communication theory and practice, can still give good advice. He points to the futility of

downward communication only, to the difference between communication and information, and to the fundamental grounding
of communication in perception, expectation, and involvement.
"The start of communication in organizations must be to get the
intended recipient himself to try to communicate" (pp. 21–22).

The only course, I think, that an administrator has open is
not to give up, to vary the message, abandon worn-out devices and
develop new ones, lower the volume of some messages and increase
it for others, and continue to try to make talking and writing count.
There are some who will never get the message. But there are more
who, complain as they may about all the junk they have to wade
through, will still approach a dean's office or a department mailbox
with the hope of getting some good word today.

Administrators working within a successful network of
handling information would be likely to make more informed decisions, to make information available to others for arriving at such
decisions, and to further a department's work by disseminating
information in a wide variety of ways.

What minimum skills should be expected of an administrator as an effective communicator?

First, an administrator should be capable of setting up an
information-gathering system that will put routinely into his or her
hands information that needs to be known and that will be capable
of finding information that might answer a specific need.

Second, an administrator must be a skilled processor of that
information, able to recognize the vital from the unnecessary, to
terminate purposeless flow, and to recognize new needs.

Third, an administrator must keep informed of what is
going on in those areas of his or her responsibility and help to keep
others similarly informed.

Fourth, an administrator must see that information gets to
others in an effective form and at strategic times.

Fifth, an administrator must be sensitive to structures, actions, and even manner that foster or get in the way of communication. Tone and gesture and timing are but a few of the particulars
that may escape attention.

Add to these the skills emphasized in this chapter: An

administrator must be able to speak and write well, or, if not, delegate those responsibilities to someone who can. And an administrator must often work against the ill effects of an excess of communication.

One last matter, a troublesome one for many administratrators: the felt need or compulsion to keep information from others. The failure to reappoint a popular teacher will do as an example. Such actions often provoke conflicts between students and faculty, the students taking exception to the loss of an apparently good person, the faculty becoming defensive even over what may have been a just decision. Very seldom are efforts made to inform students fully of the basis of the decision. Instead, the received wisdom is to say nothing and let it blow over. An administrator might better listen to John Stuart Mill (1947, p. 16) on not limiting the free expression of opinion: "If the opinion is right, they [the public] are deprived of the opportunity of exchanging error for truth; if wrong, they lose what is almost as great a benefit, the clearer perception and livelier impression of truth, produced by its collision with error." So, in this instance, if a department has judged fairly, then its judgment is affirmed in exposing it and given the wider exposure fair judgment deserves; if it has not judged fairly, then exposing that judgment is deserved and a necessary step to correcting it. To be sure, the instances are not the same. In the example I have chosen, an individual's privacy is being protected by not bringing his deficiencies before the public. But that does not secure that person's position nor does it silence doubts both about the individual's shortcomings and the department's judgment. Faced with this specific dilemma—and it is not unlike others that seem to call for the suppression or containment of information—I think the wiser course is to move in the direction of widening the public's understanding of the facts.

Dodds (1962, p. 121), commenting about communication between presidents and faculty, observes that "presidents are too inclined to withhold information when keeping a matter confidential is of no great importance and when disclosure would increase understanding and inspire confidence." Almost everything I say in this book rests upon my belief in the superiority of being open in dealing with other human beings. From that point of view, a need for secrecy is something an administrator should not surrender to very often.

In general, and not just as regards sensitive matters, I think administrators are too little inclined to let the public know what is going on, except, of course, in slick-paper, lavishly illustrated, and often deceptively written official advertisements for the institution. Nowhere is this more obvious than in higher education's relations with the press. In my twenty-five years work with the American Association of University Professors (AAUP), I have been consistently puzzled by the almost morbid fear that organization seems to have of releasing anything to a newspaper. In all my association with the AAUP, under different general secretaries and many different presidents, I have been amazed at terrible worries about stories of the organization's work getting out, when the obvious necessity was to get anyone to pay any attention to the organization at all.

Similarly within departments and colleges, the public might be much more usefully informed about the actual work going on in a college or university, but departments themselves hold back from conveying information of a positive kind and dummy up in the face of adverse publicity. University public relations offices have much in common with other PR offices, and they probably face more resistance in getting outside news media to accept stories that are the quiet news of the university. But they also face an almost reflex suspicion from administrators toward anyone coming around to find something out or to news that might in any way be unfavorable to the college.

Administrators should welcome the press, any press, including the college newspaper. Except at the higher levels, an administrator does not have a public relations branch. It might be a wise deployment of faculty energy to charge someone in every department or college with responsibilities for thinking about what might be newsworthy and finding ways to get it before the university and the larger public. For, as a general reality, I think administrators should worry more about no one's paying any attention to what they are doing than about anyone's finding out.

Since the sixties, colleges and universities have moved toward greater openness, forced by laws relating to discrimination, equal opportunity, access to records, and the like. Many departments operate under the pressure of two conflicting attitudes: that of the older faculty who accept the confidentiality of much that goes on, and that of a younger group more accepting of freer exchange of information. Administrators in such touchy matters as these must lead the way to a healthy openness in which privacy can still be respected.

A dean or department chairperson is most often recognized as the official spokesperson for a college or department. When controversies arise—the failure to give tenure to a popular faculty member, a serious charge against a faculty member or student, the cause of declining enrollments or diminishing student performance, for example—the administrator in charge has an obligation to speak out. "No comment" to a student reporter is a response both futile and unwise. Students will find out the truth or publish their version of it, which may be worse.

An administrator cannot have it both ways. If administrators want, and I think they should want, the public to know about the ordinary and extraordinary things they do, then they cannot hide from public view whatever they think might be unfavorable. The atmosphere of suspicion that excessive confidentiality breeds, the rumors that are born of secrecy, and the inhibiting of exchange of ideas and flow of information are bad in themselves. Teaching and learning are essentially open processes, and communicating is at the center of both.

➤➤-➤➤-➤➤-➤➤-➤➤-➤➤-➤➤-➤➤-➤➤

Chapter 5

Planning

➤➤-➤➤-➤➤-➤➤-➤➤-➤➤-➤➤-➤➤-➤➤-➤➤-➤➤-➤➤-➤➤-➤➤-➤➤-➤➤-➤➤-➤➤-➤➤

Looking ahead is an inescapable part of an administrator's job. Administrators may not be as preoccupied with long-range planning as they are steadily harassed with next week's meetings, next term's schedules, and next year's staffing. Faculty members are hardly into a term's work when they face demands arising from next term's or next year's responsibilities. Very little of this looking ahead is more than carrying an umbrella or reserving a table for lunch. When some central authority intrudes into it with requests for a five-year or ten-year plan, the opportunity to think big is often resisted because of the nagging obligations of thinking small.

I fear there is no easy way out. The individual student may hold off applying or enrolling, may decide to drop in or drop out at the last moment, but department chairpersons or deans have no such options. Worse, they are the ones who must remind everyone else that another term's or another year's demands must be reckoned with in advance. There are few times when anyone is free either from attending to the details of getting a class started and ended or from attending to the details of the quarter coming up. Short-range planning has a way of becoming an everyday vexation.

In almost all universities, much of this kind of looking ahead has been reduced to routine operations. The bookstore, or the registrar, or the dean sends something out with deadlines to be met, and faculty members respond as they are instructed to. Department chairpersons send reminders, try to meet deadlines on their own administrative calendars, and wish they had more time to think about what they are doing. There is little enough thinking going on in these routine operations, and the introduction of data-processing equipment to handle as well as to generate data has not particularly freed administrators or faculty to give more thought to what any of it means.

A recent article in *The Chronicle of Higher Education* (Grumbach, 1977, p. 32) contrasts the modern computer processing of student records with the simpler days when student records were kept by hand on a yellow card. Professor Grumbach so well describes a familiar modern experience that I quote the introduction at length:

> At the start of the semester, I received in my faculty mailbox a long memorandum from the provost of the university at which I teach. The provost is newly appointed, a youngish man full of ideas, eager for constructive change, altogether a fine fellow. . . . Its subject was "Verification of Student Course Enrollment." The provost wrote that, together with the president, the academic deans, and other administrative "elements" of the university, he was anxious that "steps be taken to enhance the effectiveness of the registration and billing process," which he sees as important "to insure the integrity and equality of the instructional programs." Now, this carping old fuddy-duddy could have left it all alone, even the curious suggestions of a connection between billing and teaching, but for the long listing which followed.

The "long listing" set forth the five printouts that "the computer support system" would provide during the first month of the term.

"Computer support system" characterizes the attitudes and actualities of much planning and thinking within a modern university. The computer is central; the support it gives may not be evident, nor the system it supports visibly superior to whatever it replaced. "At present," Drucker has pointed out (1970, p. 174), "the computer is the greatest possible obstacle to management information because everybody has been using it to produce tons of paper." Whether the computer realizes it or not (or cares), any piece of paper coming over any person's desk calls for some kind of response. The damn thing has to be filed, thrown away, looked at, or left on some corner of the desk until some disposition is decided upon. Computers tend to do what they can do: take in raw data and convert them into printouts. Thousands of students and hundreds of faculty and tens of thousands of credit hours, in themselves, provide an inexhaustible source of data, all of which have something to do with understanding exactly what is going on and are therefore of use in planning for either the short or long future.

The university suffers as much from its technological capabilities of quantifying information and keeping track of large numbers as it benefits from them. Though data gathering serves human needs, it also creates human vexations. Caffrey and Mosmann (1967, pp. 183–184), surveying the place of computers in the university, write: "Technically, it [the computer] is much simpler. . . . What is complex is not the machine itself but the pervasive effect it has on the organization and the society which uses it. These are human consequences, and the effects are on people and organizations. It is these things the administrator can and must understand." It is in this respect that a major and growing disjunction takes place between central administrators and those lower-echelon administrators—department and division chairpersons and even deans—who are directly responsible for the educational program. As regards long-range planning, the same disjunction exists between state governing boards and their planning functions and the institutions under their jurisdiction.

Palola (1970, p. 579) has put the matter well: "While students, faculty, legislators, and the general public are raising fundamental questions about the basic aims and purposes of higher education, the irrelevance of curriculums, and the alienation of constituencies from planning and administration, many planners at statewide and institutional levels are still almost wholly preoccupied with quantitative, physical, and fiscal problems." The offices and activities of systemwide or institutional planning are far removed from the actualities of most academic administrators. Dressel (1970, pp. 186–190), surveying the activities of university departments, felt that so little was known of management science in that domain that he had to define such terms as *program budgeting, input-output analysis, management information systems,* and *budgeting systems.* He writes (p. 190): "Departments have proved almost invulnerable to any attempt to introduce scientific management into the university."

I do not wish either to champion systematic, "scientific" planning or to defend the virtues of resisting it. Rather, my point is that, within colleges and universities, radically different conceptions of and attitudes toward planning are held by faculty and administrators at the department or division level and those at the level of university or systems planning. I shall have something to say of the latter in the discussion of long-range planning. But first, I want to address short-range planning as it affects deans and department chairpersons and the faculty they work with.

Data gathering and record keeping are part of short- and long-range planning, but they often act upon faculty members as unnecessary irritants. Consider the commonplace gathering of information about faculty workloads, which is intended to help anticipate and plan for faculty appointments in the years ahead. Such requests usually come from central offices and are couched in vocabulary and formulas puzzling, if not vexing, to the faculty. How many hours do you spend on student contact-centered instructional activities or on formal contract-supported, noninstitutionally funded research? Too often, such information is gathered without giving respondents a clear idea of its purpose and without providing feedback at a later time that might confirm that purpose.

The administrator who would foster faculty willingness to plan ahead or even to respond favorably to planning must work against redundant or seemingly unnecessary record keeping and data gathering. Reviewing routine practices and shifting responsibility for gathering data to a clerical staff are probably the first steps. Conferring with individual faculty members and calling small groups together are ways of giving tangibility to planning efforts that otherwise might seem remote or nebulous. One of the items of information a department chairperson should have is a schedule of office hours for the faculty. Given that, the chairperson can make a profitable morning's walk from office to office, transacting business when faculty members are not otherwise occupied, registering impressions of the way faculty keep or don't keep office hours, and creating an interest (amazement, even) that a chairperson would take the trouble to seek someone out. Much short-range planning that involves only a few people can be taken care of in this way.

How much formal meeting needs to take place for short-range planning? A successful administrator should probably start with the answer "As little as possible" and measure the success of any planning meeting by the amount of planning actually accomplished. If all that was accomplished is the planning of another planning session, something is wrong. Short-range planning involving an entire department can sometimes be taken care of at regular faculty meetings, but apparently simple matters brought before a group of people become complicated in almost direct proportion to the numbers involved. Prince (1970, p. 44) writes: "The basic unit of a meeting is two people. . . . In general, involvement decreases as the size of the meeting increases, and, from our experience, when more than seven people participate in a meeting it becomes difficult to use all the individuals enough to keep them involved. When meetings larger than seven seem necessary, ask yourself what the real purpose is." Better planning, as I have suggested, comes from conferring with individuals, getting key people together, and saving full meetings of the faculty for discussion and concurrence with proposals well worked out in advance.

Careful planning of meetings in advance is almost always a means of saving time. The administrator's obligation is clearly to develop and set forth in advance the necessary particulars of plans that need to be discussed and ratified. Following that, the administrator is obliged to so present them that faculty feel they have had a part in the planning and arrive at a course of action acceptable to all those involved. Kami (Ewing, 1972, p. 20), addressing business executives on "Planning: Realities versus Theory," is admirably direct in his advice: "Keep it simple." "Define your business." "Examine where you are and where you will be if you don't change."

Much of the short-range planning in an academic department falls to the administrator and his or her staff. But, in addition to these specific efforts, an administrator can do much to assist faculty in planning and carrying out their own teaching and scholarly activities. One important consideration is that the administrator examine carefully the ways in which academic routine falls upon the faculty. Is the situation, as I have described it, a continual rain of record keeping and planning obligations to be met? If so, an administrator can do a number of small things at the level of college or department functioning to facilitate faculty efforts: reduce the number of calls for routine information; maintain records so that information will be readily available for different purposes; refrain from calling meetings or asking for information at times when faculty are heavily involved meeting other obligations; keep track of committee assignments and activities to spread out and expedite necessary planning; get the most out of individuals and committees to reduce the involvement of the entire faculty; and identify short-range goals and see that they are achieved, marked off as unachievable, or turned into long-range objectives.

All these suggestions are aimed at reducing the clutter and making the most of both information gathering and planning. Bureaucracies create enough clutter in the course of ordinary daily operations. When I was directing the Project to Improve College Teaching, we generated two booklets for wide distribution to faculty members. The board could have distributed them free but decided to price them at $1 each. The booklets were well received, but the two of us who handled distribution forgot about the workings of university purchasing departments. Faculty members, shrewd enough to get their institutions to pay for copies, placed formal orders through the purchasing department, which required quadruplicate forms that may have cost almost as much as the booklets themselves. The most complex of these forms was from the state of

Texas. It required, on the same page, two affidavits. The first said, in effect, "I am authorized to sell the above-named materials"; the second, "I am the person who has signed the above." In many large institutions, even in states highly suspicious of white-collar crime, this red tape has been cut through by setting an arbitrary maximum sum—$25 or $50—for purchasing of items without having to go through all the steps perhaps appropriate to buying a piece of equipment costing $100,000. Some thoughtful business administrator suggested such a practice, and it is this kind of thoughtfulness I ask academic administrators to exercise in assisting others both in discharging daily obligations and in planning ahead.

An imaginative administrator should probably reserve a certain amount of energy, time, and risk to foster plans that develop outside the regular planning and that might be capitalized upon on the spot. An administration in which there is no room for any idea that has not gone through defined planning operations is an uncreative administration. Like the out-of-pocket grants maintained by some foundations whose main funds are tied up in long-range projects or large grants, the capital a good administrator maintains for on-the-spot ideas will probably pay dividends. There is little that is more discouraging than to be told: "It's a great idea. We'll do it next year." There are many matters that take extensive planning, require committed funds before they can get off the ground, involve bringing together the right people and freeing their time, and have to go through approval machineries characteristic of institutional functioning—so many that an administrator should be looking for ideas that can be taken up and acted upon with some dispatch. Such ideas may not be very well thought out, may promise no more than short-term or limited gains, and may entail risks of failing altogether. The short-term gains from such enterprises may be small in themselves; the long-term gains greater in demonstrating that an administrative structure is responsive and flexible.

Long-range planning has, like a magnet, its poles of attraction and repulsion. Academics share a common frustration in feeling that important business calling forth one's greatest powers and yielding equally great satisfactions never quite gets attention. Instead, one is consumed with petty details. Maybe there are no such lofty problems. Maybe they are only accessible by attention to small details. Maybe thinking big would prove as vexatious as thinking small were it done every day.

As administrators or faculty, college professors are doomed to spend hours in meetings that start and end at the low level of routines or that seem to be aimed at the high regions of policy but never get there. That is probably one reason why administrators responsible for long-range planning have difficulty in getting faculty to enter wholeheartedly into it. Most long-range planning seems to be imposed from on high, sometimes in anticipation of stringent financial times ahead, or to generate facts that have been requested by governing boards, or mandated from outside the institution by federal and state regulations.

With the growth of higher education in the sixties has come increasing attention to systems analysis and long-range planning, particularly at the state level. The literature of college and university administration in the past decade provides a running debate about the merits of various systems as well as some questioning of the basic premises that underlie planning. Shuck (1977, p. 598), for example, questions goal setting, quantification, and model building, all fundamental aspects of formal planning. "Many a faculty member has become cynical about involvement in planning when the end result seems so far from the original visions of accomplishment," he writes. "One keeps hoping that it will be remembered that obtuse protocols or symbols only vaguely resemble human activity; but somehow counting inevitably replaces reality, and one finds the planning process dealing almost solely with numbers and their relationships."

My own institution, the University of Utah, furnishes another example. Gubasta and Kaufman (1977, p. 402), staff members of the university's Office of Academic and Financial Planning, write: "Unfortunately, too much emphasis by many college and university administrations seems to have been placed on keeping pace with the state of the art in the automated aspects of these systems, with little or no attention given to the information to be generated or its possible uses." Their report describes how they adopted an institutional management information system independent of the Western Interstate Commission for Higher Education (WICHE) Resource Requirement Prediction Model, an ambitious effort to standardize data elements, definitions and procedures by the WICHE. Their *Resource Allocation and Planning Guide* developed out of attempts to ascertain the information needs of executive officers and deans and was followed by considerable efforts to explain and encourage its use. "It should be noted," the authors observed, "that even at the level of in-house development and presentation, the *Guide* was not received with overwhelming enthusiasm by all deans." By virtue of being a member of the faculty at this institution for twenty years, I can add a footnote. To my knowledge, little or no guidance resulting from this effort reached the department level, and, as far as the general faculty is concerned, the Office of Academic and Financial Planning is as remote from their daily activities as the Bureau of Business Statistics.

In calling attention to the distance between systems or institutional planning and faculty efforts, I am not denying the importance of system- or institution-wide planning activities. The duty of academic administrators may be to help bridge this distance, for chairpersons and deans to become more directly involved at this level of planning, and to see that the right questions are asked, that the necessary data are gathered, and that the data reach the right persons in a form that can be useful. The administrator might take on a further duty: that of seeing that those who contribute information are informed of results. For only by demonstrating concrete results is the administrator likely to offset suspicions as to the purposes behind such planning and raise the level of involvement and cooperation necessary to carrying out long-range plans.

Administrative leadership, vision, and skill are vital to successful centralized long-range planning but vital also to carrying out long-range planning within colleges or departments. Every academic unit should find ways of periodically backing off from everyday activities and short-range plans to consider long-range objectives. The administrator will be called upon to make physical arrangements, to offer a plan of procedure, to identify objectives, to assist in but not dominate the deliberations, and to provide the follow-up that puts plans into action.

Such long-range planning is more than a matter of scheduling faculty retreats to confront the big issues. Getting away is probably a good idea for any organization, probably better if it comes at a time other than when necessity forces it upon the group. But a good administrator has other ways of reminding a faculty that what is done day by day has long-term implications. Getting varied groups of faculty together in informal settings where the talk is deliberately shaped toward broad professional concerns is one way. Bringing in individuals who can explore far-reaching topics with the faculty is another. Asking individual faculty members to address their fellows, on topics as specific as grading practices and policies or as broad as the aims of a department of philosophy, is another possibility. Ongoing seminars involving both students and faculty, or university seminars, for example, the Columbia University seminars, are more ambitious possibilities. Finally, an administrator might recognize the human resources close at hand. A single knowledgeable faculty member commissioned to work out a specific plan of development, say, of an important aspect of the curriculum, and given a free period of time in which to do it, might accomplish more than a committee.

If any one of these approaches is to be tried and to have justifiable results, an administrator will probably have to take the lead and the risks. And if administrators do not choose any of these routes, then more obligations fall upon them to examine, ponder, and offer their own views of longer-range concerns. It is feasible and proper for an administrator to take the main responsibility here. An experienced administrator should be more aware than are individual faculty members of how things fit together and how present operations may be related to future ones. An administrator, by virtue of meetings attended, materials read, and people talked with, should be more aware of what broad changes are taking place and how institutions are meeting these changes. And, from a purely practical point of view, administrators occupy positions from which proposals can be made, actions initiated, and plans carried out.

The able administrator has the general responsibility for raising the level of discourse, both in the daily life of an academic group and on those specific occasions when a group comes together to contemplate the larger issues. If an administrator lacks eloquence, he or she should at least have command of logic, the patience to explore complex proposals, and an ability to organize and present facts and ideas and opinions in effective ways. By force of character or personality, an excellent administrator should show a concern for more than the self-interest of individual faculty members or even of a department or college. The administrator, in his or her person, must be a centering force, capable of establishing confidence that someone is absorbing and reflecting upon and putting to use the welter of particulars that surrounds everyone. The administrator's largeness of spirit, breadth of vision, wider sympathies and understanding should be reflected in informal conversation as well as in formal address. These qualities may find their most consequential form in carefully worked out written statements to faculty or to other administrators—briefs designed to set another person's analytic faculties to work, speculations sufficiently grounded to invite others to test them out, and arguments that carry conviction and win others over.

The administrator must, in short and long, be a thoughtful, reflective individual as well as an active one. Such thoughtfulness begins with philosophy. Unfortunately, that is where administrators of American colleges and universities appear weakest. No wonder institutions are so much creations of traditions and practices that cannot be shaken off, of physical facilities that define activities, of social needs and pressures, and of the necessities arising from either the presence or absence of money. In the administration of a typical American university, there is little apparent philosophy, from the president on down. Of course, there are shows of defining the university's purpose, but they are almost always rhetorical summaries of the obvious. Every state university president aspires to highest excellence in all things: arts, athletics, beautification, marching bands, continuing education, dramatics, faculty, graduate work, honors, international affairs, and on through the alphabet. Every dean will praise excellence of whatever type seems to apply to his or her college, and every department chairperson will translate the existing rhetoric into some balancing of department self-interest with operating necessitiees imposed from above.

At best, an apologist might argue that universities are pluralistic institutions and that an enunciation of the multiple responsibilities with which they have been charged is clearly sufficient as a philosophy. Colleges, being smaller, may keep more closely in touch with philosophy. Some colleges have even maintained philosophical stances that mark them as distinct institutions: St. John's, Antioch, Swarthmore, and at times some of the undergraduate colleges within the great universities. Administrators from such institutions sometimes contribute their voices to the educational dialogue, but that dialogue is a very low human buzz all but lost in the high-voltage hum emanating from big institutions.

Presidents might risk more in enunciating their own beliefs, thereby proving, if only to themselves, that they have some philosophy and distinguishing their own beliefs, if it seems necessary, from those of the institutions they represent. Dodds (1962, p. 41), calling for academic leadership from presidents, cites the careers of White, Eliot, Angell, Gilman, Harper, Wheeler, and Wilson as examples of presidents who "without exception gave educational philosophy, policy, and program top priority." In contrast, Corson (1960, pp. 60-61) estimates that a university president spends "less than one fifth of his time working on educational matters and keeping in touch with his faculty and students." With all allowances made for the plethora of onerous duties that fall to a president, there still should be room for the wise reflecting and speaking out that is essential to an institution's long-range educational goals.

The question may arise, Where do administrators get a philosophy? I fear too many would seek it out in the philosophy departments of their universities, a singularly unpromising source, these days, of a philosophy that might properly equip a dean or chairperson. Let's ask, rather, Where can administrators cultivate the habit of thinking about the goals of teaching and learning? The answer is as ancient as philosophy itself: within the self, through inner reflection stimulated and fed by outside experience. The first requisite may be developing an inner self as distinct from an administrative personality. That might come about by making the most of conversations with the many minds and selves that make up colleges and universities: students, teachers, other administrators, and all those other people who make a university function. It might also come about by reading similar discourse—reading a great deal, not only reports and charts and digested facts but Plato's dialogues, and parables about learning in many languages, and closely argued educational research. Besides reading, an indispensable aid to reflec-

tive thought is writing out one's own reflections, holding dialogue
with oneself by seeing what one can put down when forced to
enunciate an idea or set forth a principle. And what accompanies
this discoursing and reading? Time set aside for thinking. It might
be late at night or very early morning. It might be carved out at
high noon or at the cocktail hour. It might be prolonged in those
periods when the academic machinery does slow down, the midterm break, the summer. Again, such times are present in the
busiest administrator's schedule, if he or she would just begin by
jotting down in the appointment book: *Tuesday, 10–12, Myself—
thinking.*

Why do I compound the obvious difficulties of long-range
planning with demands so foreign to many administrators and
further extend the range of what we don't know in an area already
clouded by guesses? Not just because I value philosophy or even
because I would have administrators be philosophical. But for very
practical reasons of institutional efficiency. Individual thinking is
more efficient than group-think. The administrator who can privately think through the complexities of educational ideals confronting the realities of practice, the diversity of faculty and
students, and the inevitability of changing conditions is likely to
save faculty time. Instead of debating individual prejudices in group
settings, a faculty becomes a collection of individual thinkers whose
attentions are drawn to a well-defined and set-forth plan grounded
on philosophical considerations and developed with regard for the
practices necessary to teaching and learning.

This advocacy of a strong and philosophical administrative
voice in planning is not meant to stifle other voices. Teaching by
example is a powerful kind of teaching, as applicable to administrators among those they serve as to teachers among students. An
administrator who is conspicuous for thought will foster thinking
among faculty and students. Part of an administrator's reflective
thought should be directed toward bringing about reflective thought
in others. This may involve providing incentives, occasions, and
structures. It may involve bringing half a dozen people together to
face a specific problem. It may mean taking an entire college into
confidence in explaining a major change in emphasis or direction.
It will probably involve some setting forth of how discussion of a

proposal may move to consolidation of ideas and then to mode of acceptance and plan of action. It involves recognizing the variety of suspicions and misunderstandings that may arise amidst a group of people, but also acknowledging the strong possibilities for people preferring a sense of going somewhere rather than merely drifting.

There is one simple caveat. The act of reflective thinking may lead to a common kind of intellectual pride. Mated with a compulsion to put one's thoughts into action, it may engender an impatience with or even a hostility toward others' contrary ideas. The difficulty of imposing one person's ideas upon the variety of faculty members and students probably provides the best check to this kind of administrative pride. But the administrator who would feel the satisfaction of ideas leading to action must stay sensitive to the processes that human beings must go through before accepting a course of action, whether posed by the administrator or by anyone else.

One of the great losses in modern higher education is the diminishing of groups of people—faculty, administrators, students—working together. The idea of collegiality has been badly eroded by sheer size of universities and by the specialization that prevails everywhere, in small or large institutions. Administrators, not only for purposes of planning but certainly for that, have the responsibility to bring working and socializing groups into being, both for the health of teaching and learning and for the operations that support them. The feeling that any structure must be a permanent structure is a major impediment to establishing working groups among faculty and students. Mention getting informal groups of students and faculty together and visions of an administrative structure arise, killing the enthusiasm of some of the faculty, arousing the suspicions of administrators, scuttling the basic idea of getting people together for purposes of learning. For short-run objectives, fairly transitory groups can be established, flourish for as long as life is in them, be replaced by another group when that life flags.

So well established are the existing structures of university operation that attempts to alter any structure are met with a general "Why bother?" This question is answered by taking seriously the obvious facts that specialization has fragmented learning and reduced collegiality. The planning in recent years, resulting in cluster colleges and residential learning arrangements, for example, has aimed at long-range solutions. Thinking and planning need to continue to go on in these directions. But my point here is to emphasize what short-range planning might do. Given encouragement and assistance by an administrator, or, at the least by an administrator's not standing in the way, a group of faculty members might bring together some of their related courses to provide a term's or a year's integrated work for a group of students. Administrators are essential in fostering interdisciplinary work of even a modest kind. Within a large college, an imaginative administrator might even consider a purely arbitrary grouping of students and faculty into some kind of community, its numbers ranging from fifty to several hundred, which might have more purpose than the department and division groupings that now prevail.

What this would require is some short-range planning and respect for its possibilities. As I have said, little short-range group planning goes on. Individual faculty members plan for their own courses, quarter by quarter, keep track, often with the superfluous aid of the computer, of the students they are teaching, reflect occasionally on larger issues, and meet the problems that come up with both planning and not planning. But sitting down with others, students, faculty, and administrators, to work out intelligently something different from what institutional routine has set up for the year is seldom done. It is this vacuum in planning that I would like administrators to fill.

Let me offer the semblance of a design. There is a time toward the end of an academic year when the budget has been worked out, when a new quarter has a summer in front of it, when appointments have largely been made, when enrollment projections are reasonably firm—a time, in short, when administrators might contemplate the year ahead. They might get rid of ordinary business, bring some students and faculty into their deliberations, and consider the year past and the year ahead much as a teacher reflects upon the success of a class to which he or she has been fully committed. The best time to evaluate a class is right after it has been taught, when the realization of what went wrong and what went right is sharpest and when the desire to do it again and better is strongest. The academic program could benefit from similar short-range reflections about what went well this year and what can be done better next.

Such deliberation at the department level would offer short-range suggestions, identify long-range problems, stimulate actions among department administrators, faculty and students. At the actual level of teaching and learning, it might accomplish a good many small but useful things. For example, it might identify and reduce frictions between individual faculty members and students; it might bring into being such informal learning communities as I have mentioned; it might overcome barriers to communication; it might eliminate unnecessary steps in any number of routine procedures; it might foster some purposeful action on the part of individuals and groups responsible for aspects of an academic program. Its operations would have the advantage of not attempting to build anything in stone but rather a settling for mock-ups in plaster, which might in some future time be cast in more durable form. The intent would be to set aside permanence and progress and to stress spontaneity, imagination, even irresponsibility. Spring is a good time for this kind of unplanned planning.

I began this chapter by talking about the repulsion and attraction of thinking big. For some, long-range planning is futile, a waste of time. The money for grandiose plans will never arrive; no one will be able to agree, and the comfortable ruts are better than new paths anyway. Even so, the same faculty and students who accept this futility may experience some discomfort at being caught in plans and directions of someone else's devising. Moreover, the prolonged routines of teaching arouse strong desires for some evidence of accomplishments beyond those revealed in a gradebook, or through occasional visits from former students, or in the progression from assistant to associate to full professor. If one becomes a dean or chairperson, that in itself may attest to a life well spent. But whatever the visible marks of achievement, there remains a need to perceive, from time to time, learning as the grand enterprise it is. That alone heaps praise upon administrators who transcend the small by encouraging themselves and others to think big.

Chapter 6

>>>->>>->>>->>>->>>->>>->>>->>>

Keeping Sane

>>>->>>->>>->>>->>>->>>->>>->>>->>>->>>->>>->>>->>>->>>->>>->>>->>>

In face of all the obligations I've now placed upon administrators, it is clearly time to pay some attention to how an administrator might keep sane. Complete sanity is probably not as desirable in administrators as it appears—and may be too much to expect in the face of even such an incomplete list of duties and responsibilities as this:

1. Choosing the right priorities.
2. Identifying one's own strengths and weaknesses, inclinations, and aversions.
3. Developing skill and care in dealing with people.
4. Choosing faculty.
5. Delegating authority.
6. Getting the work done.
7. Getting and using and communicating information.

8. Supporting, and motivating oneself and others.
9. Planning and involving others in planning.
10. Maintaining a philosophical center.
11. Keeping the doors open.
12. Taking risks.
13. Making decisions.

Amidst all these demands, an administrator must find time to reflect upon ways of maintaining equilibrium. The suggestions in this chapter are set forth in no particular order but in sufficient number and detail to offer some hope for weathering the worst of days.

The satisfactions of administration, like those of teaching, come more often from guesses about how one has favorably affected others rather than from clear evidences of great success. A miserly attention to small gains is petty accounting of any kind, but an ability to gain satisfaction from small triumphs is clearly using one's common sense. Administrative work is sufficiently varied and detailed to afford such satisfactions if one will give it attention and not spoil small gains by wanting more. A compliment on a meeting handled with dispatch is about as good as a teacher's being praised for unraveling some concept for even a single student. The successful coaxing of an isolated faculty member into collaboration with someone else may make up for a good many hours of unsuccessful wrangling. If these small moments never come together in any larger design, well enough. If some do fit together to confirm that in one important aspect of administration or another some good things are happening, even better. Thoreau's advice is sound here: "Rescue the drowning and tie your shoestrings."

A recent survey of job satisfactions among college administrators (Solmon and Tierney, 1977) showed that deans found greatest satisfaction in the challenge and responsibility, congenial relationships, variety, and personal status that went with their jobs. While these kinds of satisfactions ranked high among the other administrators surveyed—presidents and vice-presidents of academic affairs, finance, and student affairs—all satisfactions were much greater among the higher ranks than among the deans. One hun-

dred percent of the presidents, for example, were satisfied with
fringe benefits, variety, challenge, and responsibility, and above 80
percent satisfied with salary, status, influence, congenial relationships, student relations, and even job security. I have a hunch job
satisfaction in university administration declines pretty much down
the scale of authority—hence my advice to lower-level administrators to make the most of small but tangible achievements.

A related way of finding satisfaction is to be able to perceive
one's administrative skills as embracing more than a single competence. As with winning some battles and losing others, an administrator may be very good at some things and not so good at others.
If the budget is baffling, maybe working with faculty committees
isn't. If planning tries one's patience, arguing a department's case
before the central administration may exhilarate. No one has to be
good at every aspect of a complex job, though there are certainly
limits to the number of duties that an administrator cannot carry
out congenially or very well. Administrators who recognize their
strengths and employ these strengths toward limited but tangible
achievements are likely to get enough periodic rewards to keep them
functioning well.

A third possibility is that of laughing at oneself. Considering
the things that are likely to happen on any given day, laughter can
rarely be escaped. Taking oneself less than seriously will have beneficial effects on others. Self-deprecating humor is both the most
common and most engaging kind of academic humor. Pomposity
and solemnity are ills to which higher educators are chronically
exposed. Few administrators can avoid the necessity of deflating
egos, including their own. Wit is a better means than any other.

Counseling an administrator to make the most of small
gains and resist the sting of small defeats does not diminish the
importance of keeping sane by seizing the opportunity to celebrate
many occasions. Celebrations and ceremonials are more important
to academic functioning than is commonly believed. One of the few
articles that acknowledges that fact is Mark Spilka's (1974) "Parties
and Funerals: An Academic Confession," published in *College
English*. It should be required reading for every department chairperson. The following gives something of the flavor and direction of
Professor Spilka's reflections:

My faith in communal possibilities was founded
in midwestern hospitality. As a graduate student at
Indiana, and later as a visiting professor, I had watched
James Work and others build great departments and
programs through genial, open ways. . . . I had [also]
tasted the sherry and crackers dispensed by Warner Rice
at Michigan, and had known firsthand an austerity—
indeed, a *tradition* of austerity—which New Englanders
well might envy. I found no such grimness when I came
to Brown: only an absence of official occasions, and a
laissez faire tradition by which Department members
went their own ways.

There was, in short, little communal pleasure at
Brown, though the potential for it was great and the
need for it, I felt, imperative. I did not formulate that
need in any complex way: I simply wanted to warm up
the joint with parties. It was one of several related measures—key appointments, democratic and educational re-
forms—by which I hoped to realize what every chairman
dreams about, a viable community of scholars.

We are all too clearly, all too often, simply an
aggregate of anarchic individuals—isolated cranks, lonely
specialists, posturing pundits, professional antagonists,
anxious job-seekers. How—unless we create and cultivate
tribal rites which bind us—can we hope to overcome
such abrasive aggregation? [1974, pp. 367–368, 372].

Tribal rites suggest well the kinds and uses of social occasions within a department. The personal style of a chairperson can
do much to establish and shape them, but creating a sympathetic
relationship between work and play, professional commitments and
social gatherings, depends on more than personal style. It depends
a great deal on a chairperson's recognition of the importance of this
relationship and purposeful acts to foster it. By virtue of position, a
chairperson is freed from some of the personal, intimate details of
entertaining. Instead, he or she can be host in a larger sense. With
some attention to dispelling the stuffy official air that can hang over
official functions, a sensitive chairperson can create and recognize
occasions for gathering that serve the common sanity.

A wise and successful administrator once told me, in response to my question about how he overcame the midyear blahs: "I leave." He did not mean taking a trip to the Caribbean or even to Cleveland. He meant simply leaving the scene of action for short periods; holing up in a library carrel happened to be his way of retreat. My own mental functioning has been greatly improved since I took up the practice of leaving committee meetings when they become oppressive (a liberty denied presiding officers). I make my excuses (a phone call to make, a digestive upset) and leave whatever room or building I am in. Somewhere close at hand is soil and rock and tree, and even looking out a window for five minutes can clear one's head. Leaving is excellent therapy and is as close at hand as an adjoining courtyard and as available as one's will to do it. And if everyone chose to leave at the same time? Reconvening in the open air might do wonders for debate, and in some instances not reconvening at all would serve the common good.

Thinking is greatly fostered by such leaving. Whatever the obligation immediately confronting one, one's own mental and physical obligations are often served by a shift of scene. Reflection under a tree may not be superior to reflection at one's desk. Still, it is different and closer to sanity, I think. Designating periods for reflective thought in one's appointment book should be as commonplace as scheduling meetings with the faculty.

Some hold on sanity is probably preserved by getting small chores done. In my days of full-time administrative work, I never felt as burdened by carrying home a briefcase full of things to be done as by carrying home a mind full of matters that would not fit in a briefcase. When there were too many of these matters that had to be faced or dodged again tomorrow, I experienced a consuming uneasiness. The only remedy was to get back to doing those things at hand, thus leaving some room for dealing with matters that were proving to be more intractable. This advice, as with most advice, can be carried too far. A day filled with taking care of nothing but small tasks can blight a week, and there are chores that some deep wisdom tells us should be put off. Nevertheless, what may seem like extra-human wisdom is really the very human self endorsing very human avoidances. Much of the art of administration lies in the act of facing up to things—and in recognizing those few occasions when it's better not to.

Administrators, like other desk people, vary widely in their psychic need to maintain a clean desk. Most successful ones maintain some semblance of order, both because neatness probably plays a disproportionate part in the selection of administrators and because most have supporting personnel who tidy up for them. Nevertheless, an administrative job that is being done well is probably one in which things do pile up, whether in fact on a desk or in one's mind and emotions. Periodic catching up, therefore, is a necessity for maintaining sanity. Many administrators of my acquaintance use Saturdays and Sundays as the times when they catch up. An uninterrupted morning can do wonders not only in clearing the desk but in clearing the mind. In teaching, I have experienced such clearing feelings regularly over the years, usually just after midterm. By that time, if teaching has gone as I would like it to, I have generated more ideas than I can pursue, checked out more books than I will get read, assigned more work than I will want to read and return, and gained a sense of the diversity of students with whom I'm working and of what they may accomplish. At such a point, I wrest out of my schedule some free afternoon for assessing what territory I've staked out, where I am, and what remains to be done. A feeling not only of catching up but of being in control rises up to replace the clutter and scatter. It is a good feeling, a necessary feeling. Such moments of consolidation are also a necessity to administrators, who must contend not only with their own disorder but with that created all around them.

Administrators do not have the luxury of changing courses and students at the end of each term. The work goes on, usually through the summers as well. Nevertheless, times between terms and summer recesses are times when a different order of business prevails. An administrator should take advantage of having fewer students and faculty around. At the same time, the responsibility for preserving continuity over the breaks falls heavily upon the administration. The department chairperson or dean must see to it that what has been well begun will not have to be begun again and what has been accomplished in proposals and plans will be put into practice when a term resumes.

Shifting focus can be a useful way of keeping one's administrative bearings, and it need not disrupt a daily schedule or one's long-term directions. A period of time given over to the details of revising a curriculum or working with a budget or making faculty appointments might give way to such different tasks as working with students to give them a role in the department or launching a faculty symposium to examine new developments in the discipline. The calendar of necessary duties often provides for such shifts. However they may seem to interrupt one thing with another, I think they serve to prevent obsessions from destroying effectiveness. Purposeful shifts of direction on the part of an administrator can assist in this kind of healthy change of perspective.

Advocacy of staying sane by this process does not endorse an unbalanced and nervous shifting from one thing to another. The inability to fix one's attention may be a sign that things are getting out of hand. Under such circumstances, an ability to stand back and recognize specific tasks that need to be brought to completion may be a step back to effective functioning.

Expressing one's satisfactions and frustrations can greatly improve one's outlook. Since administrators are presumably literate, I commend to them the usefulness of writing as therapy. I have already charged them with the need to be speakers and writers who can use words to set forth the purposes, directions, and means of achieving the common learning for which education institutions exist. Here I shall merely add that writing addressed to no audience but oneself can be very useful. The problems that keep one awake nights resorting to booze or books or TV as remedies may be better confronted by literally spelling them out. A written analysis of a situation, a listing of one's vexations, or a try at delineating solutions passes the time and may even hold up in the light of morning.

I am not sure how much continuing scholarship can contribute to an administrator's sanity. The long, uninterrupted hours that go with patient, exacting research are denied to most administrators. I have known a number of deans who have found the laboratory a place of refuge and healing, where apparently they were able to relieve their frustrations over not being able to get fully immersed in major research. Lewis Thomas, author of *The Lives of a Cell* and a remarkable medical administrator, has always kept a laboratory going despite the responsibilities of a variety of important academic administrative posts. Thomas observes, "It doesn't feel right to me not to have something going on in research.

I get to our laboratory for part of just about every day" (Bernstein, 1978, p. 37). Thomas is an exceptional individual. In the survey previously mentioned (Solmon and Tierney, p. 419), academic administrators at all levels were most dissatisfied with lack of leisure time and time for scholarly pursuits.

Administrative appointments tend to be for the full year rather than for the academic year; thus many administrators are deprived of those summer months in which scholarship can be brought into focus or to completion. In these times of increasingly specialized research, keeping abreast of the field may seem impossible for an administrator who stays with administration long. That may be an argument for broadening one's intellectual interests or for rotating administrative positions. Some relinquishing of ambitions as a scholar, at least for the duration of an appointment, may be an act of reason necessary to preserving one's reason. But going intellectually slack may result from too easily giving in to administrative pressures or one's own inclinations.

Teaching may be more possible to maintain for many administrators. If so, it can operate both as a stabilizing force and as a means of keeping the administrator conversant with students and learning. An experienced teacher-administrator can probably manage some undergraduate teaching and find it rewarding for both teacher and students. Whatever must come from the top of the head may have the benefit of a head stocked with diverse and interesting experiences as well as book learning. An institution gains something from having administrators willing to teach. Students who realize a dean or a department chairperson is teaching a lower-division course are complimented by the attention; faculty may perceive teaching administrators as still being colleagues. If teaching cannot be done well because of administrative pressures, however, it is better for the administrator not to teach at all or only during terms when a somewhat lighter routine makes it possible. The higher up one goes on the administrative ladder, the less likely teaching will remain a possibility, though there are still institutions in which the president regularly teaches a class.

Administrators are probably no more peripatetic than faculty members. Both turn to travel for specific academic purposes, for general broadening of perspectives, and for nothing more than rest and recreation. I think there is as much justification for professional travel for administrators as for faculty. Published scholarship still runs ahead of most scholars' ability to read it, and there is much redundancy and undisguised boredom in scholarly gatherings for the reading of papers. Published materials on the details of administration are less abundant, and finding out about what goes on outside of one's own place of operation is often a matter of talking directly with others. Travel has to be handled wisely by administrators, for it has to be paid for by catching up before and after. But, given even the change of pace that travel affords, it deserves to be mentioned as one other way of keeping an administrator healthy and alert.

Maybe the best aid to general mental health for a busy administrator is to find one's rhythm and keep it as best one can. Some administrators both are busy and must appear busy. Others work privately with intense concentration in order to maintain a more leisurely air in public. Some are early risers; others work into the early morning hours. But one cannot be in administration long and function successfully without arriving at work habits that establish a rhythm for getting things done.

The tensions that arise from hours and days of being stuck in an office or in meetings or talking with groups can best be dissipated through physical outlets, which become part of an overall rhythm. The administrator who has put together a confusing twelve-hour day may find an evening set of tennis more restful than a drink before the fire. Physical health and mental well-being go together. As persons should not be fat when taking administrative jobs, so they should not become fat in carrying them out. Jogging, lifting weights, skiing are not fads, nor are they solely means of prolonging life. Physical activities for persons in sedentary occupations—which administration too often is—are essential to performing professional responsibilities well.

Finally, the very diversity of the duties required of an administrator may aid in maintaining sanity. As administration is an art, it draws upon everything one encounters, everything one is, in arriving at praiseworthy achievements. One can find great satisfaction and an abundance of health in using everything one has, relating everything one does, to reaching the high achievements that were some part of the attraction to administration in the first place. But one can also become deranged in pursuit of an art—the artist gone mad because his conceptions ever run beyond his skills. Administrators must guard against the derangements that come slowly from years of having people not behaving as they should, of finding institutions even worse than they were envisioned. And still, if one has the patience of an artist, the care and concern for the materials with which he works, the ability to maintain a vision even in face of much that cannot be perceived clearly, I have a feeling sanity is likely to be preserved and much accomplished as well.

Chapter 7

➔➔➔➔➔➔➔➔➔➔➔➔

Getting the Most
Out of People

➔➔➔➔➔➔➔➔➔➔➔➔➔➔➔➔➔➔➔➔➔➔➔

Nothing is so necessary to administrators as an understanding of and caring for human beings. Herzberg (1976, p. 41) makes the case within the context of business and industry: "Without wisdom in the management of people today, we find blind alleys for the perplexed and pessimism for the dismayed." If this is so for corporations whose products are foodstuffs and drygoods, how much more so for educational enterprises, whose products and producers both are human beings.

Getting the most out of people is a demanding and often frustrating job. Administrators who are determined to keep people first, to support and reinforce and motivate them, to get the best out of themselves as well as others, might begin with this kind of self-examination:

- Be wary of regarding people—students, faculty, even other administrators—as intrusions upon valuable time.
- Be wary of seeing persons on the other side of the desk as adversaries likely to criticize, ask for or complain about something, create a problem, or place another demand upon your time.
- Be wary of interviews on the run, of conversations interrupted by the phone, appointments cut short because of other appointments, grievances turned off with a wave of the hand and "see me tomorrow," the important matters of dealing with people minimized under the pressure of time.
- Be wary of narrowing the range of people you deal with, of sticking with the comfortable colleagues, the administrative superior, the tractable and cooperative only.
- Be wary of excuses to keep the door closed, the phone off the hook, the question unraised, the answers slow in coming. Whenever a human being at the other end of a transaction is cut off, offense is likely to be taken.
- Be responsive to the efforts of others. Recognize, encourage, support, and thank.
- Avoid effusive and indiscriminate praise. Knowing and caring about what someone does may be the highest form of motivation.

Recognition that people come first and that the wise treatment of human beings is grounded in understanding and caring about them are the fundamentals upon which administrative excellence is built. The will to act upon such recognition must be mated with specific understanding of faculty's and students' needs (human needs, really), the different ways in which individuals develop and the satisfactions and dissatisfactions they experience in their work. The beginning of that understanding is in understanding oneself.

How one affects others is determined in large part by what one is. The administrator's art as it applies to developing his or her own self lies in bringing out and using wisely those qualities of personality and character essential to the complex task of bringing out the best in others. All those professionally engaged in "human resources management" stress the need for administrators to understand themselves and their roles, complex and changing as both most often are. McGregor (1967, pp. 58–60) suggests the use of the *Johari window* (Luft, 1962) as a means of identifying recognized and unrecognized personality traits. The window consists of four rectangles through which one views individual personality traits: The first, traits known to oneself and to others; the second, traits unknown to oneself but known to others; the third, traits unknown to others but known to oneself; and the fourth, traits unknown to both. This combination of our own insights and seeing ourselves as others see us is a means toward useful self-recognition.

The impact administrators make upon others arises both from what they are and from what they do and how they do it. The chairpersons and deans I admire most are active persons who have a way of coming around, dropping in, and taking an interest in what people are doing. How different a relationship is created from that which arises from seeing an administrator only at faculty meetings, by appointment, or at times of crisis. An administrator must be visible, in fact, or an invisible presence whose benevolences are plainly visible in specific support, encouragement, and reinforcement given to others. Confidence, energy, interest, and caring are central to making one's presence felt. Supporting, reinforcing, and motivating others must necessarily occupy a large part of an administrator's time.

In order to give conscious support to the efforts of others, an administrator must find out and keep abreast of what each one is doing. Though in large universities this may be a difficult task, it is not impossible. Where numbers are sufficiently small, a central administrator can maintain direct and continuing interest in each person. Where they become too large, the central administrator's responsibility must shift, in part, to the selection and support of subadministrators. Like an able and honest politician, an able and honest administrator must know the people being served and find ways of being accessible and useful to them.

Locked within regulations and budgets that pay little heed to faculty development, an administrator may feel impotent in trying to give tangible support to each member of a large and diverse faculty. But support may simply be a word of encouragement at the right time. It may be coming forth with assistance in advance of a faculty member's request. It may be sitting down with a group of people who are experiencing frustration with efforts of their own.

It may be locating extra funds or charting a path through a bureaucratic tangle.

An administrative position carries with it routine responsibilities for locating and identifying sources of support: keeping track of and posting fellowship, leave, and grant opportunities; reminding faculty of deadlines for sabbaticals, grant applications, and the like; nominating or identifying individuals who might receive awards, honors, or other supports. But, as academic publishing tends to narrow to a very small number of faculty, so do these kinds of opportunities, by themselves, single out a few. Beyond the routine, then, is the need for an administrator to identify faculty members in need of assistance and to devise ways of answering those needs in acceptable ways.

There is an art in providing support as in anything else. It can be a crude folk art—the squeaky wheel gets the grease—or a Machiavellian one, using support resources to play one person against another. Or it can be a wise and sensitive art in the form of quiet recognition, overt and enthusiastic approval, singling out efforts, drawing individuals into common efforts, easing frustrations, sympathizing with the ups and downs of human fortunes and development, and lending an actual helping hand. In these and many other ways an administrator is the key figure. Some years ago, I suggested creating a number of new administrative positions and offices, among which was the position of Approbation Officer or Acclaims Adjuster. It seemed to me that too many academics lived out their lives vaguely aggrieved because no one had recognized their true worth. A benevolent and respected administrator functioning as the Approbation Officer would have the sole duty to go around singling out and rewarding each of us for special virtues which had hitherto escaped notice.

Teaching and scholarship are not activities in which one can count on tangible and immediate reinforcements, though many good teachers gain and maintain competence in large part by the reinforcing behaviors of their students. Such reinforcements are not likely to be overwhelming at any time. More often, the occasional thanks, the paper well done, the sense of a whole class having been affected by a day's work or the work of a term, will have to do. The excitement of a few years' teaching may well give way to the deadening effects of repeated routines and the skepticism born of many years' practice without unmistakable signs of success. Good teachers, at any point in a career, probably proceed humbly and uncertainly. Scholarship is its own reward for the majority of university professors—or, if not, fully as dependent as teaching upon small recognitions and modest rewards.

Acknowledging these facts, the successful chairperson must think of specific ways of reinforcing teaching and scholarship, the responsibilities faculties take most seriously, and at the same time increasing respect for university service. As a beginning teacher, I was more complimented than threatened by my chairman's asking to visit a class, and I was genuinely encouraged by the conversation we had afterwards. The active interest of a chairperson in a department's teaching, extending to the visiting of classes, the discussing of courses, and the facilitating of new ventures can be a powerful way of reinforcing teaching efforts. An administrator has just as much opportunity to support and reinforce faculty scholarship. Some of the ways are simple: (1) reading what faculty members have written, for it is almost certain that few others will, (2) being able to talk about a faculty member's work, (3) letting others know what is being done, thus giving encouragement to the individual and adding to the stimulation of the others, (4) providing some of the necessaries that reduce the frustrations of scholarship. The want of a part-time secretary, the absence of someone to verify references, the need to get materials from the library are examples of simple wants that a good administrator might anticipate and provide.

Motivating faculty crucially applies to individuals who are running below expectations, their own as well as those of their administrators. In my years as an official improver of teaching, I heard almost as a chorus of administrative lament, "What can be done about the deadwood?" I once suggested a deadwood conference, one to which only certified deadwood would be invited, without, of course, their being told that that was the basis for their being chosen. Who might better discuss what causes deadwood and how it might be brought back to life? The very fact of being invited someplace and asked about something might spark some new life. Alas, no one had the courage to fund that conference.

The matter should not rest there. A president of a junior college in the Northwest is one of the few higher-level administrators of my acquaintance who doesn't seem to overemphasize the presence of deadwood on the faculty. "Sure," as I remember one conversation, "there are losers on the faculty and for as many reasons as there are cases. But there are never more than a few at a time, and I put my energy into seeing that there are plenty of the other kind and supporting them." Drucker (1970, p. 101) speaks in the same vein with respect to business organizations: "In the largest organization I know, there are not more than a dozen cases every two or three years. So this is not a large problem in numbers, but it is a big problem in impact. There is no one solution. These cases have to be handled strictly individually. They are the human problems that keep good managers awake at night. By your compassion, but also by your realism, in solving them, your organization will judge you."

I shall not attempt to identify all the types of individuals within academia who seem seriously deficient in self-motivation and whom outside motivations do not seem to affect. They include the lazy, the disheartened, the cynical, the exhausted, the physically ill, and others besides. The dean or chairperson who helps people get to where they themselves might like to go by force of example or by extension of specific support or encouragement earns my favor. But no administrator should quite give over the power he or she has to expect performance and to act against shortcomings, even while recognizing that severe problems of human behavior may defy remedy. How to judge that a faculty member needs professional psychological help and how to make that judgment known to the individual are among the most difficult responsibilities an administrator may face. The administrator who works exhaustively with these problems does so for the best of all reasons, not only trying to aid the individual but giving the student and society what they have a right to expect.

Public attacks on tenure tend to pit the protective self-interest of faculty against the powerlessness of administrators to remedy abuses. But the issue is not the colorful one of how to fire the bad guys. It is, in part, the less dramatic issue of administrative

reluctance to set minimum expectations and standards of performance and to act when those expectations and standards are violated.
The faculty member who does not show up for class, who gives bad
tests and arbitrary grades, who is shirking the hard work of scholarship and teaching will not make an administrator's lot easy. But
there is no reason for not calling such behavior to account and
trying to motivate the faculty member to a higher level of
performance.

If the tenor of this discussion makes an administrator uneasy,
then increased attention might be given to what a chairman colleague of mine calls "preventive maintenance," detecting signs of
slowing down or excessive frustrations or boredom or illness and
trying to head off the worst consequences. Positive actions of this
kind should not only be aimed at individuals but toward the well-
being and morale of the group. The kind of climate an administrator helps to create within a department or college can be a strong
source of motivation for individuals. Bringing people together often
provides direct and indirect motivation, particularly if the administrator is skillful at defining problems and adept at getting concerted action to help meet them. One faculty member hearing about
what others are doing may find that a source of motivation. Providing opportunities for faculty members to share their perspectives
on teaching with students outside the classroom can be an excellent
source of motivation for teaching. In a variety of ways, the skillful
administrator can provide the conditions and occasions by which
human beings can motivate each other.

Maintaining department harmony may be difficult today
under the strains of job insecurities and increased competition.
"Collegiality fractures under such pressures," Benezet writes (Mc-
Henry and Associates, 1977, p. 43): "factions, charges, and grievances abound." Facing such conditions, an administrator can act
as a leavening agent amidst common tensions. Professional competence is involved in being able to put down the daily gripes, antag-
onisms, and vexations of all kinds and to present a hopeful if not
benign countenance. A positive stance will be adopted and rein-
forced by assistants, office personnel, and close colleagues in ways
that work powerfully if indirectly toward getting the most out of
collegial relationships. In the midst of major setbacks, find occasions

to recognize modest achievements; in the face of defeat, make the grieving brief.

I am not inviting the false smile, the forced laugh. Nor am I advocating covering up one's anxieties with a false sense of composure or well-being. And yet, we all have some talent for restraining our most intense emotions. We may never be certain when keeping it all in or letting it all hang out is the best course, either for ourselves or for others. But as an administrator affects the attitudes and actions of others, the ability to control one's inner states as well as to declare them is a professional capability. As one might seek out pleasures to be shared, so one might deliberately reduce the outward signs of tensions that often go with administrative jobs. Forgetting, avoiding, holing up, and hunkering down are some of these behaviors. Fussing, talking things to death, and secret dealings are others.

Assisting others to find genuine pleasure—joy, even—in their work is fundamental to getting the best out of them. Argyris (1957, pp. 24–26), whose career has been devoted to linking personality development with business management, places much emphasis upon the administrator's skill in drawing upon the psychological energy individuals can give to their work. The joy of an activity that has truly fruitful outcomes is greater than the mere satisfactions that arise from reducing tensions in getting a job done. "In joy," Goldstein writes (Argyris, p. 28), "there is disequilibrium, but it is productive disequilibrium, leading toward fruitful activity and a particular kind of self-realization." For academic men and women, that kind of self-realization does not come from merely meeting classes and producing articles, but from deriving from their work a deep pleasure for which the word *joy* is not only appropriate but clinically accurate.

Being happy in one's work is not only a sign of work going well; it is an incitement to others to see that their work goes well, too. "There are two ways of managing," writes Michael J. Kami, former corporate vice-president and planning director (in Ewing, 1972, p. 27): "managing by fear and managing by enthusiasm. I believe . . . the time has come to start managing business so that it's fun. After all, you spend eight hours a day in the confines of the office; you might as well enjoy it."

Finally, getting the most out of people calls upon an administrator's capacity and willingness to exercise leadership, not the mere carrying out of duties but the establishing of a presence that leads others to extend their own efforts. In academic organizations, individuals do not so much work *for* the leader as for what the leader represents on their behalf. Such an administrative leader must be able to identify and describe clearly and persuasively common goals and to create a sense of common purposes, not easy amidst professors pursuing specialized interests and among groups of faculty and students working toward different specific goals. A talent for orchestrating the talents of others, both for quietly seeing that the work of a maximum number of individuals goes well and for making visible the collective achievements of the group is a vital talent.

As if that were not enough, administrators may, at times, have to refrain from exercising their own skills so that members of a faculty do not find themselves overly dependent and fail to develop skills in themselves. Skill in drawing upon the talents of others may, to some degree, depend upon restraint in exercising one's own talents. Actively calling for and welcoming the ideas of others is only a first step, little better than putting up a suggestion box. More to the point is identifying individuals who might welcome carrying out responsibilities. A wise administrator might assume an assisting role in carrying out another individual's ideas. For though a receptive administrator can stimulate a flow of suggestions and ideas, even more can be achieved when administrative actions make something of these ideas and openly recognize where they have come from.

Solicitous attention to the needs of individuals will not in itself distinguish an administrator as a catalyst for the efforts of a group. Driving and manipulating is even less likely to enlist the combined energies of a faculty for long. Nor can an administrator get the most from a faculty by relying upon individual faculty members to be the department's driving force or upon groups of faculty to organize themselves and function effectively. The administrator who is successful at motivating others will always move between upsetting some people by not doing enough and upsetting others by doing too much. At the least, the administrator must take actions that recognize that someone is in charge and willing to act in the group's interest. At best, he or she may see a group of people fulfill some of their highest individual aims and develop into a highly self-motivating and mutually reinforcing educational enterprise.

VIII

Chapter 8

-≫≫-≫≫-≫≫-≫≫-≫≫-≫≫-≫≫-≫≫

Identifying
Administrators

-≫≫-≫≫-≫≫-≫≫-≫≫-≫≫-≫≫-≫≫-≫≫-≫≫-≫≫-≫≫-≫≫-≫≫-≫≫-≫≫-≫≫

If we are to have decent college administration, we must choose good administrators. Such administrators must have a mastery of the details that facilitate the work of teaching and learning and be adept at getting the most out of people. The choice of college administrators is not always determined by these primary qualifications, both because of the difficulty of identifying them among the many who enter administration without previous experience and because of the conditions and attitudes that affect the selection of individuals for particular jobs.

I think there are three ruling attitudes that determine the rough sorting out of faculty members into administration. The first is the insistence that administrators come from the faculty. The second is the general disdain faculty members have toward administration. The third is coupled with the second: the tendency to regard administration as less difficult, less valuable, and much more unpleasant than either teaching or research. Together these three do more than rational choice to decide who will be administrators.

American colleges and universities have never developed anything comparable to a civil service responsible for the administrative functioning of academic programs. Nonacademic employees do fill the lower clerical ranks, but they almost always serve a former faculty member occupying the administrative position of authority. Almost all presidents (Ferrari, 1970, pp. 92–93) come from the academic ranks; eight out of ten have had college teaching experience. Drucker (1970, p. 96) asks that business managers similarly have an acquaintance with what they manage. "To manage—which means being responsible for performance and direction—one has to have a certain core of understanding." Certainly education is a distinctive and important enough enterprise that its administrators should have experience with academic matters. Yet restricting the choice of administrators to the professor narrows the range of selection, and it may stand in the way of developing and making use of administrative talent outside the professoriate. Keane (1970, pp. 56–61) and Andersen (McHenry and Associates, 1977, p. 11) are the only sources I came across in my reading to suggest that university administration might be benefited by increasing the number of administrators trained in business management.

Were there a zest for administration and general willingness to develop administrative expertise within faculty ranks, this limited choice might do. But, though faculty members will insist on having one of their own lead them and insist, too, that they have the major say in deciding who it will be, they will not easily give up their general disdain for those who accept. The many professors and administrators who contributed to Dibden's *The Academic Deanship in American Colleges and Universities* (1968) give various examples of this disdain. A then university president, Francis Horn, tells of a colleague's response to his intention of appointing a good research man and teacher to a deanship: "Why do you have to take him out of the classroom and make a dean of him?" Horn comments: "Now the implication is clear—and how many times have you heard it?—we can take second-rate academic men and make deans or administrators out of them. But the need for good administrators is just as great as for good professors" (p. 107).

College and university administrators are chiefly male. Basil (1972, p. 29) estimates that the proportion of top management positions held by women stays at about 2 percent. The same proportion probably applies to university administration. Astin and Bayer (1972, p. 118) conclude that women "have not been promoted to or asked to assume administrative leadership." The majority of college and university administrators, women or men, are probably individuals of middling achievements, competence, and prestige, measured by prevailing professorial values. We all recognize some of the types: the amiable colleague willing to take the job but not likely to threaten the faculty by making much of the position; the compromise candidate who may please no one very much but who has displeased no one either; the modestly successful teacher or scholar who can be spared for administration; the ambitious but shrewd type who will disguise his ambitions to gain the office by which he can fulfill them; the self-effacing, responsible type who ends up with minor administrative chores and who, in time, finds a regular place on an administrative career ladder; the prestigious figure willing to lend his name to the position but with no intention of becoming a skilled administrator. Excluded from administrative positions are most of those who manifest a genuine interest in having the job, who show too much respect for or too keen an apprehension of how demanding it can be, who have some signs of having genuinely tried to prepare for such a job (training or experience in education or business administration is likely to be interpreted negatively in all areas outside those schools). Despite the horror stories one still hears about administrative tyrants, I think the harsh and overbearing are outnumbered by the well-meaning but relatively unskilled, the agreeable but relatively passive. Dodds' (1962) word *caretaker* applies as well to the lower ranks of administrators as to presidents.

Now, all of the above types may include some who develop into excellent administrators and even academic leaders. Nor do I mean to slight those, not yet mentioned, who seem genuinely fitted to carry out the complex and demanding job of administration at any level. The sorting and selecting processes do single out efficient, humane, and active individuals who become effective academic leaders. They also eliminate many who might serve but lack the minimum skills or personal qualities necessary for successful administering—among them the abrasive types, who, unless they have offsetting virtues, will not be successful administrators. And confining choice to those within academic ranks assures that college chairpersons, deans, vice-presidents, and presidents will at least have an acquaintance with the particulars—teaching, research, faculty, students—that are central to higher education. Nevertheless, the forces that narrow and shape the choice of administrators call for extraordinary care in choosing from a limited stock.

What are some of the favorable signs that a member of the faculty might make a good administrator? The thirty characteristics used by the American Council on Education to evaluate candidates for its Administrative Intern Program (McIntosh and Maier, 1976, p. 90) offer sound but somewhat staggering guidance. The list, in its entirety, includes resourcefulness and adaptability, integrity and honesty, courage and commitment, ability in interpersonal relations, professionalism, assertiveness and sense of direction, organizational and analytical ability, poise and self-confidence, communication skills, vigor and capacity for work, judgment, imagination and initiative, and loyalty—as well as perseverance, breadth of interests and curiosity, intelligence, cultural level, scholarship and teaching ability, and common sense. And, in addition, sense of humor, candor and openness, motivation and enthusiasm, sense of values, sensitivity for colleagues and community, dependability, patience, sense of perspective, maturity, decisiveness, and overall standing among peers.

I cannot quarrel with the list; it has worked well for the ACE program. But my discussion will not attempt to be as inclusive. Since academic administrators come from academic ranks, it is well to begin by looking at those qualities of a scholar-teacher that might bring a candidate to a selection committee's attention. Success as a teacher may be a more favorable sign than success as a scholar, for the teacher's work is public in the same way that an administrator's is, while a scholar's work is often private. Then, too, the effective teacher has to be a motivator, just as the administrator is called upon to motivate others. That large part of a teacher's work

involving understanding of and interaction with students is not
unlike the administrator's work with faculty and others. The specialization and isolation necessary for scholarly work are not prime
requisites for carrying out administrative duties. Dodds (1962,
p. 71) mentions a number of vital differences between the demands
made upon a professor and those made upon an administrator.
"He must exchange a more regulated life of long office hours and
orderly procedures" for the freedom of the teacher-scholar. He must
"take action on a great many matters in a relatively short space of
time." He must accept "as a fact of life that for him self-realization
is attained in, and through, an organization." Though scholarship
and teaching are, ideally, complementary activities, faculty members, in fact, differ widely in their inclination to one or the other.
An inclination toward teaching may promise more for successful
administration than a commitment to scholarship. The successful
teacher must have demonstrated an ability to deal easily and honestly and effectively with people, an ability I place among the prime
requirements for a successful administrator. Moreover, excellent
teaching requires that patient attention to the details of the craft,
for the benefit of others, that I place equally high among an administrator's qualifications. Although I question the accuracy of his
observations, Salmen's (1971, p. 70) views express the common
disdain for administration: "There are few candidates for most
chairmanships. It is a duty to be accepted intermittently at a time
when it will not cause too great an interruption in research or
writing or the preparation of a course. While all senior faculty
should be willing to be chairmen, every effort should be made to
avoid interrupting a scholarly task. . . . A professor who wants
the duties of chairman either does not understand them or
should be considered as a candidate for full-time administrative
posts. Administration and scholarship or good teaching are not
compatible."

It is well to move away from these ill-considered observations
about department chairpersons. A limited but useful rule of
thumb is to look with favor upon people whom others turn to for
professional as well as personal advice. Some members of a group
are more open to others, genuinely interested in the work others
are doing, perhaps possessed of more insight into problems. Pa-

tience, an ability to reserve judgment, but a willingness to make judgments when necessary are other attributes that become apparent through personal acquaintance but that are not recorded among scholarly credentials. Even the process of formally interviewing a candidate may not be sufficient to identify such characteristics, making it more important to search beyond the visible evidence of professional competence to identify capacities for dealing successfully with people.

Confidence, particularly the quiet confidence that doesn't cast a harsh light on others' insecurities, is a favorable sign. Curiously, inside and outside academic settings, confidence and competence, qualities that would seem necessary to the performance of any responsibility, may work against a person's being selected for an administrative position. As Aristides could be too just and so be banned from Athens, so can prospective administrators show too much confidence, even that which is based upon genuine competence.

Courage is a good sign in an administrator, but it must be looked at carefully. Courage and toughness and bullheadedness can be easily confused. The courage to recognize when one is wrong, to admit mistakes rather than tough them out, is as necessary to administration as is the courage to express and argue for one's ideas, to set and pursue objectives, and to face difficult situations. Demonstrating the courage of one's convictions is generally praiseworthy, the more to be praised as those convictions are based upon judgment and wisdom.

A reputation for fairness and respect for the opinions and actions of others should be counted in favor of a prospective administrator. Students are probably more instrumental in creating such reputations than faculty. Over a number of years they see their scholar-teachers in a variety of situations in which such fairness and respect may become apparent. Department chairpersons, in particular, must not only be fair in dealing with others but must be able to convince others that they are. They must deal with the fact that what may seem fair to one person may not seem so to another.

Most administrators, I am sure, would place "tact" among those qualities one should look for in a successful administrator. I would prefer to think of it as sensitivity. There is a fine line between thinness and thickness of skin that may mark the difference between an administrator's success and failures. Success is often measured by the signals a good administrator picks up from individuals as well as from the group. Is faculty member A seriously aggrieved, and what are the causes? When is a social occasion a professional necessity rather than an optional diversion? What seemingly trivial matters of routine functioning create positive or adverse effects? Though administrators must be very sensitive in such matters, they must also have some thickness of skin to keep their nerves intact. As an administrator appears before the public, such exercise and control of sensitivity may appear as tact, the ability to spare and smooth the feelings of others, to reconcile and mediate, and to preserve the best effects of courtesy and civility.

Compassion must also be included among favorable signs. Learning is often served by error. The administrator who cannot foster the taking of risks, the willingness to expose one's ignorance, is falling short of serving the highest ends of education. And, though in the best of circumstances fairness and respect and sensitivity will do to meet instances of falling short or making mistakes, occasions will also arise in which mercy and compassion are the best course. An administrator with an absolute sense of justice is likely to have a troubled career. A broad tolerance and compassion, which recognizes the imperfections of the world and human beings, is not incompatible with respecting high standards.

It is probably not merely a favorable sign but a necessary sign that a faculty member who is moving to an administrative post be secure in what he or she is already doing. Scholarly eminence does not alone qualify a person for an administrative position, and the ranks of chairpersons and deans are filled with successful scholars who proved to be quite unsuccessful in handling administrative assignments. Nevertheless, an administrator who has not established confidence in his ability as scholar or teacher is not likely to establish confidence easily as an administrator. Administrative jobs leave little time for development of teaching and scholarship. Thus, administrative assignments may come at right or wrong times in a person's career. The wrong time is clearly when the individuals chosen have not established themselves in some solid way, which both they and those they serve highly respect. The right time is just as clearly when candidates have the security of accomplished teaching and scholarship, which both win respect and enable them to give full attention to administration.

Finally, if there is one negative capability that promises well for administrators, it is the ability to put up with petty annoyances. Faculty members who show ability to take care of the aggravating details of teaching and scholarship without letting them alter their personalities or control their lives may have administrative talent. Clean desks and cluttered ones are time-honored ways of guessing about a person's capacity for handling detail. If one has to choose, the clean desk may be a better sign, as long as it does not reveal an unhealthy compulsiveness. An administrative assistant I kept for the better part of a year kept a scrupulously clean desk. He appeared to be a whiz at taking care of details. Ask that a job be done, it was done, with a succinct memo informing all concerned and a fresh file folder in the right place in the files. Unfortunately, the compulsive neatness was gained at the price of sidestepping anything that appeared to have many parts or was messy in any way. The supposedly clean desk didn't reveal, until later, that much of the dispatch was only in the eye of the dispatcher. Before the year was out, I had to seek another assistant to take care of situations that had become unglued or that had never been stuck together in the first place.

It may be that the patience to deal with things carries over to dealing with people. The faculty member who puts up with the eccentricities and excesses of a variety of students and colleagues may be possessed of a valuable administrative talent. It may show itself in effective committee work, in bringing people together, in remaining above factions without stilling one's own voice or convictions.

These are just some of the signs that may predict administrative success. There are also unfavorable portents. Leanness and fatness, as qualities of character more than of physical appearance, are both unfavorable signs. The lean and the fat do, nevertheless, get hired regularly, lean ones usually from the top, to shape up the faculty, fat ones by colleagues, to let everyone have a fair chance at the trough. If one had to choose between lean and fat, one might opt for the supposed gregariousness that goes with an abundance of flesh. Aristotle's magnanimous man is a better model than Cassius.

Certainly secretiveness, aloofness, remoteness are bad signs. Loners may be attracted to administration and may appear to be attractive prospects, particularly where factions and favoritism have been the rule. But the useful life of administrators chosen for this reason is probably short. Few survive for very long the hatchet work required, which their temperament or ambitions made them accept. Machiavelli said men must either be caressed or annihilated in a prince's establishing dominion over a new or rebel territory and that "injuries should be done all together, so that being less tasted, they will give less offence" (1940, p. 35). But for an established republic "nothing so certainly secures to a prince the public esteem as some remarkable action or saying dictated by his regard for the public good, showing him to be magnanimous, liberal, and just" (p. 511). As venomous as academic life is sometimes described to be, its conditions more nearly approximate a stable republic than an embattled city-state. In that climate, administrators who operate too much alone may err not so much by imposing their own limited designs upon others as by depriving themselves of essential sources of information and support.

The signs of safe mediocrity are often so benign as to escape close examination. The safe candidate speaks softly, asks no important questions and essays no important answers, agrees with everyone to some degree, disagrees with no one very much. To members of a search committee, most attuned to individual likes and dislikes, such candidates have a fatal attraction. Candidates showing strength of personality or convictions tend to get eliminated early; the final choices are made from those who offer some degree of safety. Playing it safe often seems to go with blandness, a want of visible energy, which obviously does not threaten even as it does not promise much. To me, a safe candidate is likely to be the wrong candidate, not because my philosophy presses for administrators willing to take more risks and to show greater imagination but because playing it safe may have behind it a basic dishonesty or an actual want of ideas, imagination, and conviction.

Insecurity is a very bad sign in a prospective administrator, though its effects are not likely to be felt until after an appointment has been made. Insecurity is not to be confused with genuine lack of certainty about how to carry out the many responsibilities of the job. Little in the ordinary course of a faculty member's becoming an administrator for the first time gives the person much preparation or, consequently, confidence upon which competence can be built. New administrators learn about the details of the job from their predecessors, may have absorbed some style of operation from observing other administrators, but they have few measures of whether they will function well or poorly. A certain amount of insecurity may be the hallmark of a new administrator, but insecurity that has developed into defensiveness is a clear warning signal. Beware the administrator who begins in office by hiring his own personal secretary, redecorating the office, and setting up protocols disguised as management efficiency. Likely to follow are barriers to access, a breakdown in two-way communication, and increasing separation between the administrator and his public. To some degree, defensiveness is hard for a new administrator to avoid. Someone is always going to ask for something an administrator can't provide; some messages are certain to be misunderstood; some decisions to be wrong. The defensive administrator will weaken his effectiveness by being engaged in internal conflicts, too reluctant to face responsibilities, and too inclined to delegate authority to escape blame.

Excessive vanity is detectable in a prospective administrator and should be included among unfavorable signs. The higher academic administration, I think, took on the vanities of business administration in the flush times following World War II. Before that time, presidential offices maintained a decent austerity. Afterwards, the inner sanctums of high university officials became indistinguishable from executive suites of business enterprises. Rank has its privileges is the most innocent thing they say. The contrast with faculty offices is still marked, though the more lowly administrative offices, like those of department chairpersons, have been able to adopt, at an economy level, the higher administrative style.

Innocent and ubiquitous as these vanities may appear, they may reveal a more serious vanity about the nature of higher education. Administrative pomp serves neither the student nor the faculty; neither are somehow made better by occasional visits to executive suites nor are better served by officials surrounded by comparative luxury. A donor or trustee may be seduced into investment or trust by visiting a president's office that has a reasonable resemblance to his own. But within democratic institutions and amidst a constant call for funds, luxurious appointments may create adverse impressions. For the administrator who pays great attention to these things, who needs them, who gains a sense of worth from them, the effects are probably all adverse. On the one hand, self-serving and vanity, both deadly to superior administration, are encouraged. On the other hand, creature comforts and the desire to maintain them operate to make staying in office more important than doing the work well.

Some of the signals given off by individuals seeking administrative positions are so obviously unfavorable as to need little discussion. Pomposity, bluster, false modesty are as sure giveaways as obsequiousness, insipidity, and a true modesty based on lack of achievement or competence. Indecisiveness and evasion show up in personal interviews. Similarly, rigidity, ignorance, and narrowness of vision or experience do not speak well of a candidate. Finally, I look at heaviness as a generally bad sign. Heaviness is not the same as fatness, mentioned earlier in this chapter. Being heavy is inclining toward the ponderous. Gravity of demeanor and slowness of movement are outward signs of heaviness. At an extreme, all acts, ideas, feelings incline to the sitting posture. Solidity looks good at banquet tables, before boards of trustees, and in alumni magazines. But it contrasts almost everywhere with the freer, more flexible demeanor of either faculty or students. In an aspiring administrator, heaviness is a bad sign because it prematurely embraces a condition that might better be staved off. Administration as an occupation inclines toward heaviness, and only by adding leavening at the point of entry is the ultimate sinking down to be offset.

Administrators should not come from the ranks of those who take themselves too seriously. Wit and humor are not commonly found among administrators, and even the appreciation of wit and humor seems to atrophy with time in office. And yet, there is hardly anything as comic as a bureaucracy. I do not mean that administrators should not take their work seriously but that they should take it lightly also. Our language speaks favorably of possessing a light touch, of rising to the occasion and rising above the situation, of lifting our spirits, and of lightening our burdens. It is that lightness I favor; gravity will claim us soon enough.

Chapter 9

-»»-»»-»»-»»-»»-»»-»»-»»

Selecting Faculty

-»»-»»-»»-»»-»»-»»-»»-»»-»»-»»-»»-»»-»»-»»-»»-»»-»»-»»

Successful administrators are likely to be measured by the quality of their appointments, whether a president is picking vice-presidents, a dean sorting out chairpersons of departments, or department chairpersons taking chief though not sole responsibility for selecting faculty. Selecting faculty is a vital function in any college or university so this chapter will focus upon the administrator's role in that task. In most institutions, chairpersons play a major part in all the processes that lead to appointment of a faculty member. In smaller institutions, a dean or division head may discharge these responsibilities, and in some schools a central administration makes appointments. Details of actual selection processes vary with the structure and practices of an institution. But a common need exists everywhere for administrative judgment in arriving at a wise selection of faculty. What should one look for and how should one judge what one finds?

The administrator in charge has the chief responsibility for judging, from facts and figures, from an acquaintance with the profession, and from a sense of student, faculty, and institutional aims, the kinds of faculty members needed. This goes well beyond simply filling slots, though that still governs most academic hiring. It should go beyond a trading in reputation and fashion, though that, too, characterizes much of academic mobility. Wiser choices are made by careful and continuing assessment of department needs, not only for the short term but for the longer range as well. Most departments require a variety of talents for their successful functioning. Scholarship and teaching come first, but too little attention is given to the diversity within these broad terms. A scholar selected for a traditionally defined academic slot may not be as important to a department's development as a scholar who, whatever his or her specialty, might inspire scholarship in others. A teacher of recognized competence in a specific area may be less desirable than a first-rate teacher who could teach a variety of courses attractive to undergraduates. Without attention to needs that go beyond simple replacement, a department will grow sterile, find itself incapable of changing as outside conditions are sure to change. Within the range of talents to look for, besides those defined by scholarship and teaching, are administrative talents. Too many departments fail to recognize the need for faculty members who have some promise of administering effectively the many activities departments are often involved in.

How an administrator goes about identifying needs follows no prescribed path. Having put people first, the attentive chairperson will be keeping running tabs on the department's strengths and weaknesses. When vacancies arise, other members of the department and, in some institutions, other members of the administration will want to have their say. The chairperson responsible for the appointment must weigh faculty recommendations and institutional needs beyond the department's. Failing to convey effectively his or her own sense of needs is as much a shortcoming as refusing to heed advice from others.

Administrators may be expected to work closely with search committees in filling vacancies. Sommerfeld and Nagely (1974) give a good description of the organizing and functioning of such committees. Useful as they are, they do not excuse an administrator from being actively involved. Turning over an appointment to a group of specialists may unwisely narrow the choices. For a committee is unlikely to be sufficiently informed about the various needs of the department and institution that a particular appointment must meet. The informed administrator should have pondered over the strengths and weaknesses of the department, reflected upon kinds as well as degrees of excellence, and faced the facts of enrollment, budget, and changes within the institution and the profession. This kind of enlarging the vision of the faculty, vital to making good appointments, should be embraced as an administrator's responsibility at all times. Within a democratic framework, the administrator is responsible for seeing that the details of recruiting and appointing go smoothly. To faculty members, getting someone in their area who is competent but not threatening, by a process that spares them the details but gives them full voice in the decision, is the ideal. A chairperson is often caught between these faculty pressures and institutional pressures of other kinds. To some degree, the desires and efforts of both are dependent upon the market.

Locating the kind of faculty a specific department most desires usually follows practices and traditions within a discipline. Collective efforts by a faculty to keep in touch with graduate schools are often helpful, and, increasingly, departments are announcing positions in various specialized and general academic publications. Regulations and pressures from the Department of Health, Education, and Welfare (HEW) have helped move some recruiting beyond the old-boy stage. Whatever specific practices prevail, a chairperson's responsibility is still that of finding first-rate faculty instead of waiting for them to show up in the day's mail. A chairperson should always be recruiting and, in the necessary travels and correspondence that go with the office, be keeping an eye out for impressive scholars and teachers who might fit some future need.

A number of simple rules can be set forth for handling the details that go with recruiting. First, the administrator is the most likely and capable person to do the first rough screening of candidates and should remain involved in any subsequent screening. The word of an experienced chairperson may be necessary to ensure fair consideration of the unusual candidate who may not fit a narrow conception of a position. Second, the chairperson should establish a routine system for getting prompt notice back to those who are not going to be given further consideration. This is a simple courtesy, often neglected in the press of applicants in the current market—and that much more important to them. Equally important, such attention creates a favorable impression of a department, always useful in attracting faculty. Third, involving the department in the recruiting and appointing processes is an important obligation. In the present period, when appointments in some departments may be few and when anxiety about who will be kept and who won't is high, it is especially important to involve the department in these decisions. New appointments affect the lives of present faculty members. Summarizing the conditions of the market and the progress of a search, circulating dossiers, and appointing screening committees are ways the chairperson can keep the department involved.

In many departments, the ultimate decision for appointments is a peer decision; however that is managed, the chairperson is likely to have the chief role in carrying it out. At the center of appointment processes are the evaluations of candidates, for which written information and personal interviews provide the basis. Reading dossiers and letters of recommendation is somewhat like interpreting the nutritional information set forth on a breakfast-food box. Inexperienced readers do it poorly. Experience can make one too wary, cynical, or even despairing. But the advantage of having standing committees on recruitment and appointments, and chairpersons operating at the center of these actions, is the experience that can be brought to the reading of dossiers. Such experience early arrives at some things to discount or disregard and some other things to weight heavily.

In the first category are these: grades in graduate courses, graduate course work, and many letters of recommendation. Precise grades don't exist for graduate courses, and undergraduate grades within the B-to-A range do not do much to identify degrees of excellence. Graduate course work does little beyond confirming a candidate's declared area of specialization. What most hiring institutions need at the time of first appointment (and often in the future, too) is not what a typical pattern of graduate courses provides. What one might look for in course work are signs of independence and ranging that may be manifest there, for evidence of particular courses aimed at developing specific skills, and for an indication that a candidate was aware of the best faculty a graduate school offered, regardless of specialization.

Letters of recommendation should also not be taken at face value, particularly those from professors who have worked most closely with the student. This is not simply because of a general tendency to speak well of those one recommends. A dissertation director should be the best judge of a candidate, but he or she is almost certain to be the most biased judge. Professors' reputations are made and maintained by the accomplishments of their students; getting candidates placed is not only a matter of assisting them but of furthering one's own career. Professors with less acquaintance will say less, but what they say may have to be relied on more. Knowing the recommender reasonably well is very helpful, though that may merely be a way of strengthening one's own biases. For the most part, one has to develop skill in reading letters of recommendation. A formal study of such letters (Rim, 1976) showed wide disagreement among senior professors asked to rate a sample of actual letters as being favorable, indifferent or ambiguous, or unfavorable to the candidate. Rim concludes that "the reliability of letters of recommendation leaves much to be desired" (1976, p. 444).

Letters of recommendation abound in simple and complex evasions of truth. For example, a "mature scholar" probably means one who entered graduate school late, has been there a long time, and will likely go into retirement before evincing any youthful spark or brilliance. "Some signs of immaturity" most likely means that the person has hardly developed since puberty. To read that a candidate is "polite and well groomed" doubtless means that no other conspicuous trait useful to teaching and scholarship has made itself apparent. "Can't quite estimate potential" masks a strong suspicion that there may be none. "Working hard" or a "hard worker" is in the same category as "well groomed." "Thoughtful and reflective" may be a similar dodge, particularly if the person is "unusually" so. "Somewhat" and "tends toward" and "inclines to" are sign posts to pay *more* rather than *less* attention to the quality being described.

A strong brief for the candidate's narrow or specialized competence is almost always a means of covering up general deficiencies—for example, the teacher who is not a spellbinder in the lecture hall but who is very good in the seminar room or the one who has some difficulties with the general run of students but who does very well with honors groups. Negatives are to be looked at with great care, as in the above sentence: "not a spellbinder." Dullness is probably what the recommender is hinting at. Similarly, "not a profound scholar," "not a brilliant thinker," "not the most outstanding candidate" are *not* so much signs of exacting judgment as they are hints about grave deficiencies.

On the positive side, one should pay close attention to specific evidence of demonstrated competence of any kind. As teaching has gained more attention in the last decade, more reliable evidence is being included in dossiers. Student evaluations do afford more of an estimate of a teacher's performance and potential than the general statements contained in letters of reference. Materials used in the teaching of a class—course descriptions, syllabi, examinations, exercisces, means of grading—can be asked for and fairly assessed. Few departments have many faculty members patient enough to read dissertations; published articles carry the weight that someone has read them. If a candidate's written work is to be read carefully, the chairperson will probably have to do it or see that others do. For both teaching and scholarship, letters should be scrutinized for exactness of evidence: the recommender has visited classes, has examined teaching materials, has read the candidate's scholarly work. The assessments made should not be merely variants on good or bad, but specific citing of what and how well the candidate has done.

Signs of achievement at the undergraduate level commonly get overlooked or undervalued. Graduate work affords a narrow range of grades among candidates and fewer opportunities for individuals to reveal a range of interests and competence. Intellectual achievements at the undergraduate level are good signs, not only the GPA but election to local and national honor societies, awards for essays or competitions of other kinds, and publication in student magazines and newspapers. Responsible offices held in student government or achievements that indicate competence in the pursuit of academic or nonacademic interests are important. Breadth of class work and of activities outside the curriculum is extremely important, for graduate work seldom adds to a student's breadth of learning or outlook.

The administration also occupies the position through which personal information about a candidate is filtered. The old-boy system had the merit of measuring a candidate by what one person knew about another, but the attendant vices as well. The chairperson has a duty to seek out first-hand judgments of others and to use them wisely. Neither can be done solely through correspondence or over the phone. Professional meetings are of as dubious value in academia as in other professions, but they do have the function of placing those who attend in a larger frame of reference. I would not encourage administrators to become visible in the profession at the expense of their own institution's welfare, but I endorse the necessity of amplifying one's concepts of competence and excellence and of establishing a wider network for gathering information and making judgments.

At the end of the faculty selection process is the personal interview, held either off campus by the chairperson or delegated faculty or on campus with wide exposure to faculty, administrators, and, sometimes, students. Administrative judgment is essential here, for one cannot either bring in an endless run of candidates or stop at one or two and risk arousing suspicions as to how thorough a search has been made. Some administrators may be able to establish the kind of confidence or power that gains acceptance of appointments who have only been interviewed by the administrative officer. The financial investment in faculty scarcely warrants such practices, even in hard-pressed colleges. Indeed, such hiring probably proceeds more from a desire to screen out undesirables and assert authority than from other considerations. The position most administrators must take is that of leading, guiding, and involving others in appointments.

Conducting and arranging for interviews is an important administrative skill. Slave markets, the annual hiring activities of professional associations, are the chief scenes of off-campus interviews. The complaints that candidates make about these proceedings include failure to keep appointments, mass interviews, drunkenness,

belligerence, cynicism, and general rudeness. However confined
these abuses are to a few errant interviewers, the temptation is
always there to "test" a candidate by affecting some extreme manner—anger, toughness, cynicism, ennui. But one's aim in an interview should be the same as the candidate's: to see the other person
as he or she is. Putting a prospective colleague at ease, then, is a
first responsibility of an interviewer.

Many of the characteristics that apply to successful teaching,
the kind that genuinely "bring out" students, apply to successful
interviewing. Recognizing the context in which interviews are being
held is a first point. If chairpersons at national meetings feel
harassed, candidates feel much more so. If a candidate has been
brought to a campus for interviews, the small courtesies of furnish-
ing a reasonable schedule, extending an invitation to relax and get
located, inquiring about the candidate's desires and preferences are
not mere graces; they are the beginning of establishing confidence
and respect that move toward candor and useful disclosure.

Ideally, the interview should afford some variety of contexts and situations. A single interview on a tight schedule in a hotel
room may be better than nothing, but it is chiefly useful as a screening device. In such interviews, an administrator should probably
be looking for favorable impressions rather than for definitive signs
of excellence. What is there about the way candidates conduct
themselves, answer questions, volunteer information, relax or remain
ill at ease, show enthusiasm or provoke interest that may carry over
to successful scholarship and teaching? In addition to how candidates respond to administrators' questions, what questions do they
themselves introduce? What evasions or preoccupations appear?
What ability to pursue a line of questioning? What grace in sustain-
ing conversation? A good interview should range beyond the expected questions about degrees, areas of specialization, plans for
scholarship, preferences in teaching, and the like into questions
about why the prospect has chosen teaching and scholarship in the
first place and how his or her professional life may relate to personal
and community concerns.

Trick questions, trapping questions, playing devil's advocate are
most often—maybe always—to be avoided. At the least, they may
be misinterpreted; at the worst, they are discourteous and exercise

the unfair advantage of a person in power over one who is obviously powerless. Questions about a candidate's personal life, religious or political sympathies, interests and avocations are avoided by some administrators. These kinds of questions are important, and part of an interviewer's skill should be knowing how to separate questions that expand one's knowledge of a candidate from those that violate privacy. For what a person is cannot be deduced from, any more than it can be determined by, only the graduate work and professional experience that prepare one for a job.

Part of the purpose of the personal interview is to get a glimpse of the candidate as a person as well as a scholar. The aim is to furnish better judgment as to how such things as physical presence, manner of speaking, personal values, and the like may relate to teaching skill, scholarly competence, and working with others. When the judgment is right, both the institution and the newly employed professor benefit from the understanding established during the interviewing process.

The on-campus interview furnishes important opportunities besides those of talking with faculty and administrators. Though it is not a common practice, candidates should be given opportunities to be seen as teachers. Most beginning appointments emphasize teaching, and arranging for a candidate to teach or participate in teaching one or more classes is not difficult. The chairperson is centrally involved here, in ascertaining the best kind of arrangements, in assuring fairness to both the candidate and the department, and in observing the candidate as teacher and adding his observations to those of the students and faculty. In addition, the chairperson should see that the candidate engages in exchanges of ideas and opinions both within areas of specialization and outside those areas, has opportunities to react to the kind of department, university, students, and community being considered, and is placed in informal, relaxed settings as well as in formal situations.

A certain degree of formality is inescapable in arranging interviews on campus. But interviews need not be wooden; requiring or inviting the candidate to read a formal paper in his or her area of specialization is probably a bad practice. Even in departments that give scholarship high priority, few members of the department are ever required to thus formally assail their colleagues. Giving candidates a chance, not to be grilled, but to engage in give and take on matters that interest them, including but not confined to their academic expertise, is a better practice.

In all these processes, chairpersons have responsibility for saving faculty members' time as well as for placing demands upon them. The saving comes in handling efficiently such simple matters as giving ample notice, of relating campus visits to faculty members' other obligations, and of clearing spots in a calendar for the various necessary meetings. The interviews concluded, the chairperson can save much time by ascertaining informally but judiciously where the sentiment of the faculty lies. Face to face conversations with faculty are best, held openly and in advance of the formal convening that may be required for appointments. Having done such sounding out in advance, the chairperson can save more time by coming to the department with firm recommendations or, if not that, firm procedures for moving toward specific recommendations. The administrator's power of recommending can be both used and abused. Nevertheless, it seems to me to be indispensable to good administration and quite compatible with the faculty's desire to have full opportunity to deliberate and come to consensus about important decisions within a department. The decision to recommend one candidate over another is one of the most important decisions chairpersons make. Failure to recommend is almost always a failure to face responsibilities.

In properly administered institutions, making academic appointments is a responsibility administrators share with the faculty. Leadership is as important here as in any other aspect of an administrator's work. The art of administration lies in the good judgment and wise decisions the administrator draws from the faculty. The position of administrator gives that person the vantage point from which proposals and recommendations can be made and objections and reservations voiced. As it is difficult to make appointments to which an administrator is strongly opposed, so does the strength of appointments in the future reflect back upon the administrator's positive actions.

One final caveat to the administrator about selecting faculty: concern for making good appointments does not end when an appointment is finally made. Certainly, after the often exhausting work that leads to successful appointments, both the administrator and the faculty need a break. But to make that break the end of dealing with personnel matters is less than wise. For the chairperson, selecting faculty is only the first step in helping them develop and in deploying their talents. Together, these responsibilities are the most satisfying aspect of a chairperson's job. If one has gone to the pains of seeking out and scrutinizing and deliberating over potentially excellent faculty, additional pains should be taken to assist new faculty in reaching their potential.

Similarly, what one learns in the handling of vital personnel matters, not only appointments but reviews for retention, promotion, tenure, and salaries, should not be lost in the relief that accompanies getting onerous jobs done. Administrators, like new faculty appointments, seldom have access to systematic on-the-job training. Both must learn by experience, and one season of working at the vital task of building and renewing a staff is invaluable experience in developing one's skills as a personnel officer. Nor should that learning be confined to the administrator. Sometime after the hectic pace of recruiting and reviewing has slackened, it will be the chairperson's duty to call faculty together to analyze with them what has worked and what has not worked and to review personnel needs in the future.

Obviously, an administrator in charge of a department or division or college must accept the wide and complex functions of a personnel officer. Only in large departments can this task be specifically assigned to someone else or its functions distributed among various faculty members and assistants. Even then, the central administrator has just that much more responsibility in selecting those who will carry out personnel functions. In short, there is no evading the necessity of developing the skill and judgment that go into choosing and maintaining department and college staff, faculty, administration, and nonacademic personnel alike.

Chapter 10

+>>>+>>>+>>>+>>>+>>>+>>>+>>>+>>>+>>>

Serving and Leading

+>>>+>>>+>>>+>>>+>>>+>>>+>>>+>>>+>>>+>>>+>>>+>>>+>>>+>>>+>>>+>>>+>>>

To both serve and lead: that seems to be the paradox many college administrators face. In a general way, the academic person—faculty member or administrator—accepts the idea of service: to the institution, to the discipline, to students, to the public, to knowledge and learning, to human reason. But confusion is likely to result amidst so many different perceptions of service. Also, in the college and university reward system, service ranks definitely below teaching and research as prime responsibilities. Administration is equated with service, and since teaching and research are clearly separated from administration, faculty have another reason for losing sight of the fact that both teaching and research are valuable services, too.

The paradoxical nature of serving and leading may explain faculty's acceptance of administrative authority as long as it clearly appears to be serving prime faculty interests. Reluctance to accept that authority may increase as administrators emphasize specific

113

faculty service roles. Many administrators, too, feel they have been taken away from their primary interests—teaching and research—so they themselves may be reluctant to stress the importance of service. Administrators aspiring both to serve and to lead, then, must overcome some hostility to authority exercised even in behalf of those activities they and the faculty most prize.

Academic persons are not peculiar in these respects. McClelland's (1975, pp. 265–266) examination of power has expressed the administrator's dilemma well: "In real life many leaders balance on a knife edge between expressing personal dominance and exercising the more socialized type of leadership. They show first one face of power, then the other. The reason lies in the simple fact that even if the man is a socialized leader, he must take initiative in helping the group he leads to form its goals. How much initiative he should take, how persuasive he should attempt to be, and at what point his clear enthusiasm for central goals becomes personal authoritarian insistence that those goals are the right ones whatever the members of the group may think, are all questions calculated to frustrate the well-intentioned leader. If he takes no initiative, he is no leader. If he takes too much, he becomes a dictator."

McClelland is only stating in an analytic way some implications of Lord Acton's "Power tends to corrupt; absolute power corrupts absolutely." Analyzing the exercise of power and the safeguards against abuse of power within American institutions, he concludes: "A Martian observer might conclude that as a nation we are excessively, almost obsessively worried about the abuse of power" (p. 267). Though he is speaking of power within a different context, McClelland's generalization describes a well-established attitude within colleges and universities: "People are suspicious of a man who wants power, even if he wants it for sincere and altruistic reasons. He is often socially conditioned to be suspicious of himself" (p. 256).

Robert Greenleaf, whose career has been devoted to management research, observes: "We live at a time when holders of power are suspect and actions that stem from authority are questioned" (1977, p. 5). Greenleaf's book *Servant Leadership* is a wise and powerful plea for leaders who truly serve and more serving institutions. He expresses his hopes thus: "A new moral principle is emerging which holds that the only authority deserving one's allegiance is that which is freely and knowingly granted by the led to the leader in response to, and in proportion to, the clearly evident servant stature of the leader. Those who choose to follow this principle will not casually accept the authority of existing institutions. *Rather, they will freely respond only to individuals who are chosen as leaders because they are proven and trusted as servants"* (p. 10).

Only very isolated administrators can escape daily (if not hourly) reminders of their serving roles. But, in a large and important way, some administrators may separate that kind of serving (even as they may accept it) from serving within an organized administrative structure. For them, primary responsibility is to the administrative superior and to the authority of the institution. Strict adherence to this pyramid of authority model is much less common in higher education than in public school education, where it almost everywhere prevails. College professors, jealous of an independence lodged in their specialized scholarly competence, reject the simple authoritarian administrative model. And administrators who see themselves as primarily serving those in authority above them are not likely to become leaders of the faculty.

Rejecting the administrative model in which responsibilities are defined chiefly from the top down is a good safeguard against administrators who respond to being given power by abusing it. But the ill effects of the conferral of power can manifest themselves at every level of collegiate administration. Given the fact that shared authority is widely accepted by collegiate institutions, faculties probably deserve the administrators they get, particularly the ones they keep. Since faculty members have other than administrative duties and are often preoccupied with other matters, authoritarian, even tyrannical administrators may arise and establish themselves so firmly that only concerted action by a majority of faculty members can dislodge them. Whether one reasons from the chronic need for leadership or from the adverse affects of the abuse of power, much thought must be given to how a prospective administrator will exercise leadership and respond to the conferral of authority and power.

In business management, persuasive voices have argued for the superior effectiveness of cooperative management over authoritarian management. Shared authority is firmly established within higher education. This kind of management is based on a belief that human resources are the vital center of any institution's success. Greenleaf (1977, p. 49) asserts that "caring for persons, the more able and the less able serving each other, is the rock upon which a good society is built." Books advising about this kind of leadership are as abundant as those about decision making, organization structure, management objectives, and other aspects of administration. Tead's *The Art of Leadership* (1935) is still an excellent source of common sense advice. Though some later books (Adair, 1973; Bird, 1940; Gouldner, 1950; Gibb, 1969) cast doubt upon identifying specific leadership traits, most would accept Adair's definition of leadership as "that part of a manager's job concerned with getting the best contribution from those for whose work he is responsible" (p. 19). Tead acknowledges the arbitrariness of any list of essential qualities; however, he places emphasis upon a leader's having intelligence, integrity, and decisiveness, physical and nervous energy, enthusiasm for his work, and personal qualities that can influence others. "The writers and scholars of business agree," Levinson (1968, p. 116) writes. "They, too, call for the generalist who is a specialist in managing people, in creating a climate in which people can do their best, and who will be judged by what his followers do."

Leaders who truly serve will neither abuse the exercising of authority nor avoid it. Finding a course between these extremes, and between the views held by many faculty that only these extremes are possible, is not easy. One's psychological makeup may incline a person in one direction or the other. Pressures from the diverse individuals one works with will push in both directions. With one set of individuals and conditions, firm exercise of authority may be necessary. With another, a more relaxed hold on authority will prove to be a better course.

As authoritarian academic administrators are resented most, I shall address the following questions directly to administrators who have some feeling that they may be too much under the influence of their own authority:

1. Do you resent, however slightly, letters and direct address that do not get your title or position quite right?
2. Do you establish a correct form of address among those distinctly inferior to you in position?

3. Do you resent your opinions or judgments being questioned by your peers?
4. Do you welcome opportunities to set people straight?
5. Are you bothered because decisions that might have been made by you are made by your superiors?
6. Do you take pride in making the big decisions, especially those that involve a show of muscle?
7. Do you find it difficult to laugh at mistakes you have made?
8. Do you use your position to gain favors from others?
9. Do you shrug off or allot to others the detail work of administration?
10. Do you justify brusqueness, haste, and lateness by dwelling upon how busy you are?
11. Do you cut through discussion, limit debate, and insist on sticking by the rules and regulations?
12. Do you find yourself creating new rules and regulations?
13. Does your exercising of authority carry over into your domestic and social life?

Affirmative answers to the preceding questions are signs that a need to exercise authority is eroding more effective and congenial ways of leadership. In contrast, a reluctance to take on authority or to exercise it fruitfully may underlie affirmative answers to the following questions:

1. Do you find it necessary to talk to someone about every decision you make?
2. Do you generally make the same decision anyway?
3. Do you find the same matters coming up again and again and not apparently getting settled?
4. Do you put controversial matters last on the agenda? Set confrontations aside? Avoid confrontations?
5. Do you find yourself talking excessively at meetings at which decisions are to be made?
6. Do you refer a great many matters to higher authority?
7. Do you answer questions at far greater length than is necessary?
8. Do more and more matters of minor importance pile up on your desk?

9. Do you get in trouble because you've said one thing to one person and a conflicting thing to another?
10. Do you become increasingly critical of the decisions others have made?
11. Do you find yourself promising things to people and finding you can't come through with them?
12. Do you spend conspicuous amounts of time regretting your decisions or worrying about consequences?

Delegating authority is a special aspect of leadership calling for a special ability. "By common agreement among presidents," Dodds (1962, p. 74) writes, "their most prevalent administrative weakness is inability to delegate work to others." To delegate authority well, one must have successfully resolved prior questions of exercising too much or too little of one's own authority. In addition, one must have a pretty sure sense of what cannot or should not be done by someone else, some security in what one can and must do, and a large amount of trust that there are important matters that can be done as well or better by someone else.

Administrative models vary in the degree of reliance placed upon delegated authority. One common academic model is that of a principal administrator—dean or department chairperson—assisted by one or more associate or assistant administrators. It is a reasonably satisfactory model, which often works well within informally run departments or colleges. The assistant takes over when the dean or chairperson is off campus; at other times, specific responsibilities are left to the associates and assistants. Sometimes the assistant is merely at the elbow of the chairperson, a kind of listening ear and responding voice, or even a real partner in everything that needs attending to.

The chief administrator in most college settings has the responsibility for choosing assisting administrative personnel and even deciding upon how they are to be used and what authority is to be delegated to them. Administrators usually insist on selecting assistants with whom they are congenial and who are in agreement with the chief administrator's mode of operation. Commonly, the chief likes to take care of the big-think problems and leave the lesser responsibilities to others. There is some sense in that arrangement and some danger. In the first place, individuals willing to do the grubby work may be hard to find, and those who can be found may be no better at that than at more important work. In the second place, the hope that such persons exist may foster a delusion on the part of deans or chairpersons that they can escape the dirty work altogether.

A better mode of operation, I think, is to work out with a prospective assistant some division of important as well as unimportant matters. If an assistant stays over a period of time, the opportunity to handle a variety of important responsibilities will provide excellent training for greater administrative responsibilities. Some matters, particularly those that directly affect a faculty member's welfare, cannot easily be transferred to an assistant. Faculties probably accept most the authority of those whom they have collectively placed in office. That does not mean that the duties of associate deans or assistant chairpersons should not bring them into touch with, even conflict with, faculty. But the dean or chairperson should not use them to avoid his own exercising of leadership.

As clearly as possible, a dean or chairperson should establish with assisting administrators and with those affected by administrative decisions the lines of authority, the limits of authority, and the responsibility of authority. In small departments, there is probably little delegation of authority, though the department may run as much by consensus of the faculty as do large departments. In large departments within large universities, functions within a department become differentiated, and the number of subadministrators grows: directors of undergraduate programs, of graduate studies, of research, of honors, of personnel, of separate subject matter emphases and programs. In a large college of arts and letters or letters and science, an associate dean may become almost wholly responsible for a large and well-defined area of that college's work. The dean becomes a kind of supervisory figure responsible for overall budgeting, common policies, decisions at the highest level, coordination of the work of the separate colleges, and mediation between a central administration and separate faculties and their students. A department chairperson of a very large department may assume a similar role.

I do not intend to enter into an abstract debate here about

the virtues of centralized as against decentralized administration, though I strongly favor any efforts made to give some coherence to the university and to maintain collegial relationships among disciplines. Rather, I wish to consider administrators' conduct in the face of realities. Presidents and deans and department chairpersons will continue to have responsibility for giving unity and direction to the entities they administer. Delegating authority to vice-presidents or associate deans or subadministrators within departments does threaten unity even as it serves the functioning of parts. If the chief administrator cannot provide an overall sense of direction, cannot set priorities and reconcile major conflicts, he or she is, in my opinion, failing to carry out a main administrative responsibility. For though it is highly desirable to delegate authority to first-rate individuals and to give them maximum freedom to carry out their responsibilities, that course may not always arrive at the highest ends. The success of the parts as defined by each of those in charge may not be an accurate measure of the success of the whole. Many administrators fail to see that a chief administrator's success depends not only upon the ability to work through subordinate administrators to achieve comprehensive goals but also upon the ability to establish and maintain a comprehensive and unifying point of view.

Modern universities have been pulled more and more away from centralized authority to college and department autonomy. Presidents have been frequently charged with a failure of leadership, though I think they have a clearer idea than other administrators of their responsibility for providing central goals and directions and of their dependence upon an administrative structure to carry them out. "We cannot conceive," Dodds writes (1962, p. 2) "that the president, as the number one man in the organization, can delegate to academic vice-presidents, provosts, and deans an overriding responsibility toward the university's primary role." Chief administrators at all levels must work to keep overall aims in touch with and in harmony with the aims and operations of the separate parts. At the level of daily operations, that means, most of all, being careful in choosing those to whom authority is delegated, allowing them to draw fully upon their initiative, imagination and competences, and defining at the outset and periodically thereafter how the scope of their authority relates to overall aims.

Since teaching and scholarship are department responsibilities, deans may take on ceremonial functions or become mere conduits between a central administration and departments. With large colleges under their jurisdiction, they may delegate much authority and get out of touch with both faculty and students. As heads of small colleges, they may be overly protective of the interests of a separate college. Perhaps deans experience the most difficulty in operating as academic middlemen. It may be necessary for deans (as well as for other chief administrators) to identify particular responsibilities that fall under their sway. A dean might devote his major energies to the undergraduate program, working directly to effect changes in department programs as well as through the assistant deans and department chairpersons. A chairperson might become, for a time, the head of remedial mathematics and again give his major energies to working directly with the program as well as with the subadministrators to whom that responsibility has been delegated. The dangers are clearly those of neglecting the overall welfare and of encroaching upon authority previously delegated. The first danger can be offset most effectively by using the overall administrative authority and energy not only to affect an individual program but to set a model of how a part is related to the whole. Indeed, this exercise of authority may be vital to shoring up some sagging part of the operation or deliberately moving one part of a college or department in a new and promising direction. As to the other danger, a dean or department chairperson should accept the fact that being in charge is a license to override authority that has been delegated by the dean or chairperson in the first place. A clumsy interference or second-guessing that saps the confidence of associates and assistants is unwise if not intolerable. But the assertion of central authority in the light of overall needs or changing conditions or poor performance is an obligation that goes with being in charge.

Delegating authority to subadministrators necessitates a fair and penetrating assessment of administrative functioning. A grave lack of colleges and universities is the lack of any systematic evaluation of administrators: presidents, vice-presidents, deans, and chairpersons. In theory, these responsible administrators all keep tabs on the administrators reporting directly to them. In practice, very seldom are administrative officers subjected to the kind of annual review and recommendation that takes place for the faculty. In the present climate of mandatory accountability and of annual review of faculty, of student evaluations of teachers, and of peer evaluations of research, administrators' performances need to be evaluated in systematic ways. Deans do subject department chairpersons to periodic review, which may involve both students and faculty in the process. Less frequently, deans receive a similar kind of review. During my twenty-three years at the University of Utah, I have observed only one attempt to involve the faculty in a formal review of deans or higher administrative officers. Ehrle (1975) describes a good design for evaluating department chairpersons, which embraces uniform procedures, a written set of performance criteria, and basic input from faculty on performance with respect to communication, decision making, operations, delegation of responsibility, problem solving, relations with students and colleagues, and public relations.

Administrators should be at work devising systematic ways to evaluate their own performances as well as those of persons to whom they have delegated authority. Student evaluation of teachers furnishes an obvious model for gathering regular, objective, processable data from those an administrator specifically serves. Interviews with faculty and students, taped if necessary to preserve anonymity, are another way of getting necessary input. Teams of visitors comprised of those inside and outside the institution are other means of assessing departmental quality and administrative performance as well. Serving purely at the pleasure of an administrative hierarchy and being subject to no more scrutiny than the off-hand one of a higher-ranking administrator are ill-advised practices.

Successful delegation of authority rests upon the quality of persons selected to carry out that authority. The best person in any administrative job, even the humblest one, is a whole person. Too often, the problem of dealing with poor teachers or disaffected scholars is solved by assigning them to minor administrative functions. Similarly, such positions often go to individuals who like to do clerical chores. Neither category provides a good source of sub-administrators. Sooner rather than later, the seemingly nonpersonal details—scheduling, ordering books and supplies, gathering statistics, and the like—become personal, and, unless the person handling supplies and rooms and figures has a keen sense of how these impinge upon individuals, administrators in charge are going to be constantly harassed by vexations not of their own making. These negative reasons aside, the positive reasons are that human beings affect the mechanics of the operation in which they are enmeshed. A secretary who smiles willingly is worth two who don't; the graduate director who excites, invites, and continues to welcome students who must come to him on essentially trivial matters is worth three who make routine confrontations painful. The presence of a maximum number of individuals—all, if possible—who can overcome the sterility of bureaucratic education and who can reduce the disparity between what higher education professes and how it creeps along is the first essential of a first-rate administrative staff.

Finally, delegating authority well requires that an administrator recognize when a bad appointment has been made and take steps toward a remedy. With administrative appointments as with faculty appointments, the responsible administrator must see that both the individual and the institution are treated fairly. Severance of an individual without proper cause is obviously unfair to the individual. But failure to sever with good cause is unfair to the institution and to the public that institution serves. The administrator has the responsibility of judging performance on the basis of carefully established expectations and of working with the person to achieve them. In most processes of evaluation, the administrator will have to draw upon the judgments of others, screen out personal pique and prejudice, and recommend or act to retain or dismiss. Being indecisive in these matters is as common a fault as being too hasty.

Maybe the best training for acting wisely and forcefully in matters involving faculty tenure is acting thus with respect to administrative appointments that do not carry tenure. Every administrator should establish annual review for all subadministrative positions. Whether that review is more exhaustive than the administrator's own review may be defined by a university's or a department's regulations. Many such positions are appointments by the administrator, and therefore the person appointed expects to serve at the administrator's pleasure. Commitments to such positions may match the term in office of a chairperson or dean. No commitment should be such that obvious failure to meet expectations cannot be acted upon. The skilled administrator must have the judgment, the persuasive powers, and the abilities that go with attracting good people into subadministrative positions but must also have the candor, the tact, and the decisiveness to remove people who have not worked out. These are elementary facts of successful administration. The worst of administrative mistakes is to find oneself arbitrarily defending one's appointments. Rarely is a person in a subadministrative capacity irreplaceable. Rarely is energy worth expending in defending an appointment against faculty opposition or fairly raised questions of competence.

An ability to handle disagreements and complaints is as important for the administrator in charge as for those in assisting positions. The best stance is to accept all disagreements as honest ones, all complaints as legitimate. The fact that disagreements may contain a fair measure of dishonesty, ranging from ignorance of fact to the harboring of sinister motives, and that complaints may range from petty annoyances to long-suffered ills should count for little with the wise administrator. Yet administrators commonly react foolishly to disagreements and complaints. One wrong tack assumes that the person or persons have no right to disagree or complain, haven't fairly or completely assessed the situation, or have taken the wrong course in complaining or haven't filled out the proper forms or gone through the proper channels. Another foolish tack is to assume, if not say publicly, that human beings can never agree, will always complain. Disagreements and complaints should not be taken lightly. As long as one person entertains them, they are important to that person and, therefore, important to the administrator who must hear them.

Delegating authority, then, is like exercising one's own authority. Without attention to the details of how authority is being received, without a willingness to encourage the taking of responsibilities that go with authority and to modify the exercise of authority in behalf of serving a collective good, without a steady attention to relating parts to the whole, the administrator's central duty of both serving and leading is not being done as it should be. As this chapter began by drawing upon a management expert's enunciation of "servant-leadership," so will it end with a similar observation drawn from the psychological aspects of management. Levinson (1968, p. 58) concludes that "he who would lead must follow. That is, he must understand the values and expectations of his followers. Unless he does, he will be unable to win their consent. Without consent, he cannot lead."

Chapter 11

->>>->>>->>>->>>->>>->>>->>>->>>

Making Decisions

->>>->>>->>>->>>->>>->>>->>>->>>->>>->>>->>>->>>->>>->>>->>>->>>

The willingness to make decisions may be one of the distinguishing characteristics of an administrator; making wise decisions the mark of an able administrator. There is no magic in making right decisions. During a term of office, every administrator makes many decisions, some of which turn out to be right. One always hopes the right decisions outnumber the wrong ones, or that the right ones are about matters of great consequence. There is some security in making many decisions. Only an accumulation of bad decisions is likely to scuttle a college administrator. A good run of right decisions may set up a dean for life.

In most collegiate situations, the decisions for which an administrator has sole responsibility are relatively few. Those vexing personnel decisions—appointment, retention, promotion, and tenure —as well as major decisions involving curriculums, policies, and future directions are most often group decisions. Millett (1968, p. 5) is right, I think, when he says: "The prevailing expectation today is that the collective faculty in a college or university will enjoy 'shared authority' with the administration in decision making about the institution." A dean or chairperson plays an important part in decisions reached by the college or department and is chiefly responsible for seeing that such decisions are made according to defined regulations or practices, but the decision is the adminis- trator's responsibility. An administrator's skill may be most im- portant in bringing a group to the point of deciding.

The chairperson of a department, for example, is clearly responsible for seeing that members of a department receive suf- ficient information of a kind necessary to reaching a good decision. This responsibility is almost always greater than merely making information available, just as it must always fall short of ensuring that each faculty member thoroughly digests and judiciously con- siders that information. Nevertheless, a chairperson can do much to see that documents are in the hands of faculty members; that they are there in sufficient time to be digested; that ample time is given for discussion; that discussion, like discussion in a good class, is not dominated by a few; and that the wider knowledge and perspective a chairperson may possess are legitimately brought to bear on the discussion.

A common failing in bringing a department or college faculty together to make decisions is that of not recognizing the importance of decision making at lower levels or among smaller bodies. The committee system is of fundamental importance in decision making. For, if committees are sufficiently representative and well chosen, debates that would tie up a larger body for days can be resolved in an afternoon. When such committees are able to reach firm decisions, it is likely that decision making can be facili- tated in the larger body. The responsible administrator pursues a careful but forceful path. The way committees bring recommenda- tions to a larger body tells much about how they conduct necessary business. If a committee tends toward weakly supported or poorly defined recommendations, if committee business always has to be repeated in the larger body, if committee decisions are frequently reversed, the administrator has strong indications that the com- mittee is not an effective decision-making body. The administrator's decision becomes one of finding out what is going on and of assisting the committee in its decision-making processes or of reconstituting a committee or shifting its responsibilities.

Fostering and guiding decisions, at times pushing groups, large and small, to reach them, call for great tact as well as other skills. On the one hand, the responsible administrator cannot be too obtrusive lest he or she be accused of manipulating or coercing the group; on the other hand, to be too passive may be interpreted as evading responsibilities. To some parties to a decision, arriving at a tough decision with some dispatch may appear to be just what an administrator should do. To others (often those on the losing side) such action may appear to be hasty and ill advised.

But more disaffecting to almost everyone are the failures to make decisions when decisions are needed and expected. Not every gathering of academic personnel need involve decisions, and yet few do not involve some clarifying of issues, defining of problems, and expression of ideas that, sooner or later, require the group to make choices. As too many meetings are a bane of academic existence, no administrator can afford to have many meetings that do not result in tangible accomplishments. One of the commonest and most satisfying of accomplishments is the reaching of decisions, in small matters as well as large.

Dealing wisely with both winners and losers in a decision is another skill an administrator has to develop. Anticipating how decisions may affect members of a department or a department's operations is the beginning of developing that skill. In most instances, once decisions have been made the responsibility for seeing that they are carried out falls squarely upon the administrator. The fact that much decision making in colleges and universities requires consensus or discussion and vote does not remove decision-making responsibilities from the chairperson or dean or higher officers.

The important decisions for which administrative officers are solely responsible are not likely to constitute a majority of decisions reached. For a chairperson of a department, salary decisions, faculty schedules, some personnel matters, and some matters of organizational functioning may cover most of these decisions. A dean's responsibilities are comparable, though salary decisions may be replaced by decisions affecting budget allocations, and personnel matters may be confined to the appointing of chairpersons and other such administrative officers. This is not meant to slight the many decisions an administrative leader will make toward establishing goals, instituting changes, and affecting many important educational matters. But most of these matters eventually will become subjects for group decision. As Jones (1957, p. 125) has said of the business executive: "Gaining acceptance of the decisions he has made is just as essential to the company's welfare as making the decisions in the first place." In all decision making, administrators often proceed through consultation and advice. Like Machiavelli's prince, an administrator "ought to be a great asker, and a patient hearer of the truth about those things of which he has inquired" (1940, p. 88).

One last point concerning those decisions for which administrators have final responsibility. In the atmosphere of collegial decision making that prevails in higher education, too many administrators may seem to respect consultation and advice but play a heavy hand in the actual decision. In the appointment of chairpersons, for example, deans may assert too heavily the technical right to appoint in the face of the obviously important role played by the faculty. Presidents and vice-presidents may do the same in the appointment of deans. At one time I kept a file of presidential appointments by boards of trustees that were made with little regard for consulting the faculty or in sharp contradiction of advice from screening committees, or through decisions reached outside formally defined regulations. In all such instances, some submerged need to assert power seemed to be at work. Perhaps it is again as Machiavelli said: "A prince who is not wise himself cannot be well advised."

Whether the decision is an individual one or a group one for which the person in charge has responsibility, the best stance for decision making is the willingness to face things squarely. I do not believe that facing up to things can be divided into being able to face the little things but not the big ones or, conversely, being able to come to grips with important decisions but letting the smaller ones slide. I think facing up to things is very much a matter of the whole personality and character of an individual. As I stressed at the beginning of this book, the ability to do small things well, including making lesser decisions well, is often the mark of a successful administrator. I do not know whether there is a transfer of learning from deciding little things to deciding large. Tead (1935, p. 126) apparently believes there is and advocates acquiring a habit of decisiveness by "making up your mind promptly on small things. Acquire the habit of selecting your choices firmly and then dropping all other possible alternatives from your mind."

Perhaps much of making decisions is habitual or becomes so for the good administrator, particularly as habits apply to small decisions. The successful administrator simply cannot survive if every small decision involves a labored process. Decisions of any kind profit from the mere fact of being made. "The leader must not only be decisive," Tead (1935, p. 124) writes, "he must impress his followers with the fact that a decision has been reached and that hesitation, vacillation, and questioning are over." Tough decisions put off do not become easier. Occasionally, with luck, events will fall out that make tough decisions unnecessary. But even one such event may seriously impair an administrator's functioning in that other decisions may be put off in hopes of that unlikely but possible resolution. With a more ordinary kind of luck, delay only increases anxieties, enlarges the impact of speculation and rumor, and puts off the kind of satisfying actions that can go forward even from unsettling decisions.

Unpleasant tasks that have to be performed are not really decisions, though they may involve some summoning of will to do what one must do. The chairperson with an alcoholic full professor may not be forced into making one crucial decision; more likely, he faces day by day the necessity of dealing with a complex human problem. This may involve many momentary decisions to forget about or grapple with some consequence of the problem, but only a climactic event—that on a given day, for example, Professor X has assaulted the dean—will set in motion actions toward a major decision. I am not counseling avoidance until circumstances force a decision; my general advice is just the opposite. But I am saying that some of the complex and distressing problems of dealing with people are not ones that can be resolved by an administrator's decision. Or, to illustrate from the trifling side of administrative duties, an administrator isn't really involved in decision making in carrying out most routine operations. One develops habits that make the carrying out of many routine details automatic.

New administrators should especially resist the temptation to agonize over decisions. Agonizing has its attractions: it is the self-sacrificing price one pays for being an administrator; it is the anguished apology for having risen out of the ranks; it is an excuse for bad decisions. As I think about it, the agony of decisions may indicate the insufficiencies of an administrator rather than the strengths. I am not talking about the genuine chronic agony that brings on ulcers and other anxiety-bred illnesses. Such mental and physical ills should, in themselves, keep persons from being attracted to administration. Rather, I am talking about administrators for whom agonizing decisions are seemingly quite compatible with a cheery countenance, a kind of badge worn on the sleeve mainly to convince themselves and the world how tough it is to be an administrator and how much, therefore, everyone owes to those who are willing to bear it. There is too much phoniness in such gestures, too much self-deceit and deception of others. It might be better for administrators to measure their success as decision makers by the small number of agonizing decisions they can honestly bring to mind.

To recommend minimizing the anguish that can accompany tough decisions is not to condone a callousness that would set aside all sympathy with persons who may be adversely affected by a decision. Rather, it is to ask for an unsentimental compassion, the kind of effective compassion that does not allow problems to go unattended until only a harsh resolution, an agonizing decision, is necessary. Careful attention to the well-being of persons served by administrators may forestall those decisions that bring anguish to the person affected, whether or not the anguish is shared by the administrator. Systematic, forthright, and openly conveyed assessment of performance can help avoid having to agonize over this kind of decision.

Those agonizing decisions that may involve conflicts between defenders of strongly held positions may also be made less agonizing by anticipation and prompt action. Conflicts long prolonged are worse than those that come to firm resolutions. Waffling now is likely to lead to more complex waffling later; bringing matters to a decision and making that decision may spare everyone some agony.

The diffusion of academic authority has surely diminished

the number of decisions for which any administrator takes full responsibility. Enarson, writing in 1962 (in Dibden, 1968, p. 67), says flatly that a dean "is not the decision maker, but rather a skillful mechanic in superintending the machinery of decisions." The remark is not meant to slight the importance of deans, though the tone as well as substance, appearing frequently in the literature, does much to explain the presence of those administrators who settle for efficient mechanical functioning. One could view the academic vice-president as a similar mechanic seeing that the dean's machinery runs properly. Stroup (1966, p. 103) is more precise when he observes: "Although decision making is a specialized function of administration, it is diffused through the various levels of the hierarchy of the college. The bulk of decisions, however, are performed in the lower-status offices. . . . the more important and generalized decisions are made in the upper levels of the hierarchy." At all levels of administration, decisions, large and small, have to be made, are made, and the decision maker, regardless of how mechanical he feels, should bear the responsibility.

A most common complaint against administrators, an inescapable fact of working, within bureaucracies, is that important decisions are often reached in private by those within the power structure and made to appear to be decisions by the group. Often members of the group are involved in a meaningless display of gathering opinion, holding discussions, and providing feedback for a decision that has already been reached. Such charges are hard to prove, just as such complaints are hard to put to rest. Few important issues proceed on a precise time schedule and go through open discussion and debate with enough individuals closely involved to satisfy everyone that the final decision is solely the result of these processes. Administrators are in touch with many matters affecting the college or university earlier than faculty and remain in touch with decision making at the upper levels in a way individual faculty members do not. Where trust does not exist, suspicions can and do arise. Nevertheless, those who must make decisions should do some simple things to offset the possibility that large numbers of faculty will think decisions are being made in advance and covered over with token involvement.

The best direct advice to administrators is clearly not to

arrive at fixed positions beforehand that will determine the outcome of decisions regardless of what others say or do. If a decision has been reached but that decision needs to be confirmed by a group, then that point should be clearly made. If the decision is an administrator's solely and within his powers, then he should be prepared to stand by it as his own and be judged by its outcomes. Faculty involvement should never be token involvement, for the consequences of genuinely involving faculty are greater than those of the decision reached. "Unless major segments of the academic community feel that they are part of the decision-making process, they do not gain a real sense of community" (Perkins, 1973, p. 69).

A secondary piece of advice is to be clear and forthright about how decisions are to be made, who will ultimately make them, what part the opinions and judgments of others will play in them, and when they have to be made. Opportunities to discuss issues with administrative officials who are key figures in an ultimate decision are often useful. An administrator at a lower level may have to bring about such opportunities, even against resistance from those having greater authority, who may like to limit exposure of any debatable issue. At times, a lower-level administrator may have to decide whether to withhold or voice his own doubts about the wisdom of decisions made at a higher level. If one's doubts are strong enough to voice, they should not just be communicated downward in the authority chain; they should also be directed toward the responsible authority above.

Lower-level administrators (and almost everyone is lower than someone else) may find it convenient to refer all tough decisions (those that may affect an individual department member adversely, for example) to a higher level of authority. "Gee," the plaint goes, "I'd like to do something about raises, but the dean's putting on the squeeze." The dean won't take the rap because it's the academic vice-president's fault, only he's under the thumb of the office of budget, and they are just carrying out the mandate of the president, and the president has a board to please, and the board the legislature, and the legislature (theoretically, at least) you and me. So blaming someone else seems to have a way of coming back to rest upon oneself.

We have discussed some of the many decisions that are not

the sole responsibility of an administrator. But there are decisions that are, indeed, a single administrator's, however the decision may be influenced by others above and below. The wise administrator should probably welcome those decisions for which he or she can clearly be responsible rather than develop a habit of referring every decision to some other level. Such acceptance of responsibility does much to establish the trust and confidence necessary to administering well. If most of these decisions turn out well, the administrator's position is bound to be enhanced. If they turn out as they are likely to—some good and some bad—trust and confidence may still be shown toward the administrator's decisiveness.

Tead (1935, p. 126) has written that "for a leader to find himself called upon too frequently for decisions is usually prima facie evidence that the ordinary course of operating activities has not been well laid out." In my own experience, an unsatisfactory delegation of authority or poor choice of individuals for administrative assignments may multiply the decisions a principal administrator has to make. A person uncertain of authority may hesitate to follow or enforce even clearly established policies and thereby refer to a decision-making level matters that should be taken care of routinely. A failure of those delegated authority to take action or to carry out policies may push decision making to a higher level. A careful administrator may have to encourage subordinates to make decisions, to back them in such decisions, to praise the good decisions and be generous toward the poor ones, and to move decisively when inabilities in decision making call a person's competence into question.

One can imagine an academic institution in which decisions are reached quickly and directly. Visiting some campuses during the sixties, I saw some examples of feverishly expeditious decision making. At one of the new institutions within the New York State University system, I met a string of administrators who spent a large part of their time on the phone giving instant decisions on big-money questions. "If he won't take fifteen thou, try eighteen. . . . We'll go as high as a million and a half and worry about the rest later. . . . tell the piker it's the whole package or none." These were unusual years. The normal pace of academic life works against hasty decisions.

Considering the bureaucratic organization, the need for collegial consultation, and the sensitivity of conflicting constituencies, I have always been more surprised at decisions reached promptly than at those that dragged on a long time. But the difficulty of arriving at decisions seems to put more pressure on administrators to move processes along. Expediting can be done with fairness to the complexities and importance of the issues.

Ordinary delays for which no one is precisely responsible are not the same as intentional delays. Some administrators may resort to stalling a decision, hoping that a shift of opinion may incline things in the direction desired. Delaying tactics may, at times, assist a department in cooling passions so that a judicious decision can be reached. Almost always, such actions pit the administrator's judgment against that of a sizable portion of the group. It is a delicate and dangerous position to maintain. The best course is to be honest about one's motive for counseling delay. The worst is to argue reasons for delay that the group finds spurious or to practice self-deceits to justify delay.

The adverse effects of delaying decisions almost always outweigh the beneficial ones. For, if nothing else, people served by administrators want and deserve some sense of direction and movement in the work they do. Decisions need to be made, if only as punctuation points to mark the progress of teaching and learning— more complex matters, even, than the structure of an English sentence. When I first became an English department chairman, I received a number of calls, usually at the lunch hour when I was brown-bagging it to catch up on the day's work, requesting the truth about disputed points of grammar. Now, grammar was never my strong point, and though I would occasionally catch an easy one that I could be decisive about, most often I would have to paw around among books on my shelves or refer the caller to one of our experts on the subject in question. Too often, I tried to give explanations when what the caller wanted was affirmation. If my immediate grasp of a disputed point agreed with that of the caller, I could take care of the matter in minutes and receive profuse thanks for my kindness and praise for my competence. If it did not, no amount of explanation seemed to suffice.

So, I learned to be decisive. "Sir or Ma'am," I'd say,

whether I knew or not, "Clearly in that construction, the singular is called for." And if I were asked, as I often was, "Who says so?" I'd raise the volume and lower the pitch of my voice and say, "*I* say so, and *I*'m the Head of the English Department at the University of Utah." It seemed to work, not because of the powers residing in me or in my office but because a clear decision had been made and someone was willing to stand by it.

Chapter 12

-»»-»»-»»-»»-»»-»»-»»-»»

Complex Skills for Complex Tasks

-»»-»»-»»-»»-»»-»»-»»-»»-»»-»»-»»-»»-»»-»»-»»-»»-»»-»»

As the preceding chapters do not purport to cover all the details of administration, so will this concluding chapter discuss only a few of the complex skills necessary to three broad and complex tasks. These are the care and feeding of faculty, developing an administrative style, and keeping the collective conscience.

First, the care and feeding of faculty. Much has already been said in this book about relationships between administrators and faculty. Without repeating earlier contexts, I wish to focus here upon some of the sources of chronic friction: workload and class assignments, salary, advancement, and job security. Administrators also confront the sensitivities of faculty with respect to grants and fellowships, recognitions and awards, relationships among colleagues and with other administrators, opportunities for research and travel, career development within the university, and even in such classroom matters as making and giving tests, assigning texts, and grading. Within the diversity of American colleges and universities, the autonomy granted to faculty and the authority of administrators both vary widely. But everywhere administrators have some say about what faculty members do and about what value is placed on their services. Herein lies the source of most faculty-administrative frictions, not only because the issues relate to job satisfaction and economic security but because they affect ideas of self-worth as well.

Consider the role of the administrator in establishing workload and class assignments. Few administrators at any level can escape being caught by the pull of an institution toward greater workloads and the pressure from a faculty for smaller. Unfortunately, no one, anywhere, knows how many students and how many classes constitute a fair workload, much less knows what may best suit an individual professor. The American Association of University Professors (AAUP), in its "Statement on Faculty Workload" (1970, pp. 30–32), did bravely say:

> The following maximum workload limits are necessary for any institution of higher education seriously intending to achieve and sustain an adequately high level of faculty effectiveness in teaching and scholarship:
> *For undergraduate instruction, a teaching load of twelve hours per week, with no more than six separate course preparations during the academic year.*
> *For instruction partly or entirely at the graduate level, a teaching load of nine hours per week.*

These are useful guidelines, but across the range of collegiate institutions workloads are both smaller and larger than these suggested norms.

The subtleties and complexities that underlie and define faculty workload are no more than hinted at in the AAUP statement. Kolstoe (1975, p. 46) conveys something of these: "The chief function of a university is still the pursuit of knowledge, and this fact is recognized by administrators fully as much and perhaps even more so than by academics. A consequence of this condition is the striking of an uncomfortable compromise between administrators and scholars which pleases neither perfectly; so it is, therefore, workable. This agreement recognizes that creative work knows no time constraints. Therefore, the right of scholars to set their own working hours subject to the dictates of no one is strictly observed. This pleases the scholars but not the managers. In return, professors are required to teach a certain number of hours per week. This satisfies the administrators and is tolerated as a profound but necessary nuisance by the professors. Thus a delicate balance is struck between the professors' accountability to the institution and to the scholarly discipline which enslaves them. Their workload is an extended tightwire act between the two."

The chairperson is the one who most walks the tightrope. The basic balancing act is how to get all the classes staffed within the budget and how to maintain equity of treatment among faculty members doing different things at varying levels of experience and competence. Or, to put it more succinctly, how to keep everyone reasonably busy and reasonably happy.

Although administrators sometimes find themselves working with generous and tolerant faculties, most faculties get visibly upset when wide differences appear in the number of hours professors teach. Institutional regulations may assist the administrator by mandating uniform workloads; or, within prestigious institutions, custom may sanction seeming inequities between those in the upper and lower ranks. Collective bargaining has also moved toward regularizing workloads. But the chairperson is still the key administrator, in a majority of institutions, who must find ways of helping keep the college solvent and the faculty happy.

As a beginning, an administrator may go beyond the assistance provided by regulations and custom and keep a strict accounting for each professor of the number of hours taught each term and each year, the number of students, and the number of different preparations—the basic measures that define quantity of work. This accounting should include released time, time in which the faculty member is freed from the classroom to engage in other equally valuable services. From an accurate record of these basic facts, a chairperson can adjust workloads to make the most of faculty availability, strengths, and preferences and still maintain equity.

Workload distinctions do not apply only to number of classes and students and preparations but also to level, kind and time of classes, assistance provided or not provided, and even rooms and location on campus or within a building. The administrator is faced with faculty whim, petulance, fear, ignorance, vanity, and plain cussedness along with many good reasons that argue for special treatment. The only recourse is for chairpersons to develop in themselves and the faculty a sensitive understanding of the problems. On one hand, a chairperson must display a willingness to accommodate for good reason, but, on the other hand, show a determination to stand firm against abuse. Winning respect for these positions, a chairperson may be able to keep faculty sufficiently informed and develop a sense of common purpose so that negotiating over workloads becomes an opportunity to promote understanding rather than an occasion for confrontation. Scheduling is linked to workload and class assignments and, as I pointed out earlier, is one of those seemingly routine tasks that is too important to be completely turned over to someone else.

Setting salaries is often the most personally troubling part of working with a department's or college's budget, and budget responsibilities are regarded by many administrators as the most disagreeable aspect of their work. Practices vary widely. Administrators in institutions with firm salary schedules fixed by a central agency may have the easiest time of it, along with those departments that make salary determinations the responsibility of a faculty committee.

Advice here applies to administrators who have full responsibility and little assistance. Determining the prevailing temper of the faculty with regard to openness or privacy in salary figures is one first move, though federal regulations may limit open disclosure. Most departments incline toward privacy. A chairperson must find out and be guided by the prevailing view and, even then, try to respect the sensitivities of those who may be in the minority. What dollar amounts faculty members receive as base pay or as increases may not be as important as whether their expectations are met and they are assured of fair treatment with respect to other faculty members. Lean budget years and fat ones become known to faculty members well before individual salaries are fixed. A chairperson can honestly share with the faculty grievances that are institutionwide and work with the faculty to lift the college's general salary levels to those of comparable schools. Where the chairperson is on the spot is in disappointing expectations based on a faculty member's knowledge of last year's salary and guesses about how much others receive. In general, I think promotions and notable achievements should be generously rewarded, even at the price of having to squeeze the budget in other ways.

I think it wise (in these days it may be unavoidable) to keep faculty members informed about the overall budget situation and about their own salary prospects. Letting each faculty member know a proposed salary figure while it is still subject to change may anticipate and forestall grievances. This figure can be arrived at only after the chairperson knows the general budget for the coming year and has communicated the basic facts about the overall financial picture to the faculty. It should take into consideration general cost-of-living and merit increases, specific achievements of the faculty member during the year, promotions in rank, and acknowledgment of inequities or special treatment in the past. And it should guard against being ruled by or seeming to be ruled by: What have you done lately? Few things are more dispiriting to senior faculty members than to find salary increases diminishing because an administrator can save money by paring percentage increases of higher salaries or because scholarship is going into more sustained work that will not appear as so many articles a year. Department chairpersons also need to guard against those money-saving but personally unjust weightings of faculty need and circumstance: Professor A is an unmarried woman and therefore needs less to get by on, while Professor B is a married man with a large family. Present day administrators are restrained from such practices both by the weight of public opinion and by federal regulations.

In the end, the salary figure a department chairperson proposes should represent his or her best judgment as to an equitable figure and respect the faculty member's best judgment as to whether it meets expectations. In my experience, giving a proposed figure and offering a genuine chance for negotiation has been a way of forestalling disagreements. Disagreements that do arise often have good reasons behind them and may cause some adjustments to be made rather than dissatisfactions lived with.

The college and university reward system, which includes not only salaries but advancements in rank and achievement of tenure, is a source of chronic faculty complaint, even though its general structure, through the years, has been created and sustained by the faculty. Administrators at all levels have to live with the reward system, see that its procedures are properly carried out, and often attempt to clarify and defend it.

In universities, a main source of friction lies in a general failure to recognize the diversity of valuable services performed by a faculty. The inherited reward system continues to place greatest value upon formal research following a scientific model—a system ill suited to multiversities embracing such diverse functions as training for the professions, preparing teachers for public schools, fostering the performing arts, embracing general and continuing education, and offering training in almost as many practical as theoretical skills. And since the multiversities dominate higher education, even less diversified colleges feel the effect of conflicts within the reward system. Presidents hold a misguided conception of excellence if they set the tone of an institution in accordance with major research universities despite the obvious fact that their university embraces colleges and departments engaged in other equally important educational services. Few universities in this country escape performing these services, and, though they do not attract federal funds in support of research, they earn the vital tangible and intangible support of a local community. The many faculty members basically and honorably engaged in nonresearch activities should not be judged by inappropriate standards. Clearly, it is a prime obligation of administrators to assist others to recognize the conflicts I have merely sketched above. Beyond that, administrators have a major role in clarifying to the faculty the expectations placed upon them and the standards by which they will be judged.

Since administrators work directly with the reward system, whether as academic vice-presidents, deans, or chairpersons, they must take the lead in seeing that it fairly reflects the institution's multiple objectives and values. Deans and chairpersons may, indeed, find themselves defending individual faculty members from their own colleagues in cases in which an excellent service is being performed that may not fit a narrow disciplinary perspective of a faculty. Chairpersons probably have the greatest opportunity for maintaining both excellence and morale in recognizing and fostering diversity. It falls to the chairperson to ease up on a teaching load in order for a professor to carry out a valuable work of scholarship, or to persuade a professor to slight personal scholarship to undertake a temporary administrative job, or to be firm about a faculty member's laziness disguised as doing one's own work at home. These kinds of things need to be done without incurring jealousies of other faculty members or raising suspicions about the arbitrariness or motives behind one's actions.

Working with a reward system that to many faculty members is ill fitting at best, that poses for the untenured a constant threat to job security, that arouses competition, fear, jealousy, and anger is as complex as any task administrators face. For, in addition to the major problems I have sketched, there are many other ways in which the reward system may favorably or unfavorably affect notions of self-worth central to the well-being and performance of faculty. This is where chairing comes closest to parenting, where praise is better than blame, freeing and challenging and pointing the way better than disciplining and restricting and holding by the hand. Caring and seeking to understand should distinguish a chairperson's office far more than exerting authority.

The specific ways an administrator carries out the many complex obligations a position demands are probably inseparable from his or her style of operation. Yet some administrators, like some teachers, are uncomfortable about emphasizing style. If there is a prevailing style for administrators, it is conservative. I wish it were not so, just as I wish more "art" could enliven and enlighten present administrative work. The duty of conserving may seem to fall more upon administrators than upon anyone else. Students are transient; faculty thoughts and passions are loosely tied to the administrative functioning of an institution; someone has to see that things continue to work. And yet, administrators probably do not arrive at a conservative stance or a styleless demeanor out of thoughtful choice. More often, they adapt to their surroundings. The administrative position goes to the one who owns the suit, but after that, grooming becomes an accepted part of fitting into the environment. Clothes and grooming are, to be sure, but an indication of the conservative administrative style. The more important characteristics are, at one extreme, the judicious weighing of complex issues as necessary preparation for wise decisions and actions and, at the other extreme, not speaking one's mind, not sticking one's neck out, waffling and evading and retreating into the anonymous authority and protection of an administrative office and traditional and institutional practices.

But even supposing, as I do, that the way colleges and universities are run, the nature of the selection processes, and the lack of conscious attention to administration as an art incline administrators toward a conservative stance, need they be devoid of style? My answer is clearly no. But offering advice about developing a style risks being misunderstood with respect to both the nature of style and its importance. Ideally, style should arise from *what* a person *is* as much as from *how* he or she *does* things. If an administrator has confidence, a curious and imaginative outlook on the world, and a responsiveness to other human beings, that administrator is likely to have a style. It may be devoid of self-consciousness and yet clearly mark for others a distinct way of conducting oneself. The dean I remember who was complimented for "always being himself" had style. His bearing, demeanor, and actions affected no style, but being himself was a distinctive and admired attribute, perhaps more so among administrators who often felt it necessary to strike an administrative pose.

A person devoid of style may think of it as decoration. A newly appointed administrator may attempt to take on style the way one buys a coordinated leisure suit when he decides to take on leisure. The development of an administrative style probably has to begin with recognition of style as other than affectation, more than fashion, and capable of being developed as part of one's professional competence. Slavish and stereotyped attention to style leads to foppery, disregard for style to boorishness.

My observation of current administrators leads me to believe that many choose low visibility as an operating mode and that some confuse it with style. The administrator does not have the luxury of choosing to be invisible; an administrative office demands a presence, however much or little it exerts itself. There are many ways of not being very visible: not being around, not being responsible, not interacting with others. But there is a difference between an administrator who, assessing his or her personal assets, preferences, and strengths, decides to cultivate a low-profile style and one who simply drifts into low visibility or who chooses it as an obvious way of avoiding trouble.

I am not advocating a computer readout that picks the administrative style best suited to the job at hand, but I am averring that administrators have the duty to give attention to the manner in which they carry out administrative work. Yes, this may involve some rooting out of personal mannerisms—it may be useful not to be as garrulous as one customarily is. Yes, this may involve some conscious attention to ways of putting people at their ease, of drawing them out, of developing not mere stylistic gestures but ways of relating to others. Yes, this may involve a display of energy, when the mind and body are not really so disposed, for the purpose of communicating to others a vigor, a buoyancy in carrying out a task that may raise other people's energy levels.

These suggestions are not meant to encourage eccentricities, which can easily become hallmarks of a conspicuous administrative style. Enough of these go undetected, and too many probably deserve more to be eradicated than cultivated. More important, eccentricities are at the far reaches of style. Chomping powerful cigars or erupting on schedule are more defects of character than manifestations of personal style. This discussion is not a brief for acquiring style as a simple personal accoutrement; rather it is an argument for style as necessary to carrying out complex and important professional tasks.

For example, one of those vital tasks of administration is to capitalize on the diversity of talents within a faculty and yet to organize and unify that diversity toward fulfilling overall objectives of learning and scholarship. Department organization both facilitates and inhibits the carrying out of this task (see Dressel, Johnson, and Marcus, 1970; McHenry and Associates, 1977). Some departments exist chiefly as a number of persons doing pretty much as they please within an agreed-upon discipline, while others make the most of collegiality both with respect to teaching and scholarship. It is not only administrative action but administrative style that encourages learned and learning individuals to work together. The health of a department may be a direct reflection of the chairperson's style.

I hope these remarks about administrative style are not misinterpreted. I share McGregor's ambivalence toward the term (1967, p. 68): "For reasons unknown to me I find the word 'style,' applied as it here is to managerial behavior, unattractive. But I have been unable to find another term in common use that conveys my intent as well." We all have had too much of an acquaintance with managers, supervisors, administrators to deny that style is part of their effect upon us. And where we recognize a distinctive style, we would probably say, with McGregor, "it has emerged as a result of his lifetime of coping with reality" (p. 58). Finally, most administrators are uncomfortable in talking about style because it seems to place an extra demand upon them, one which cannot easily be defined or met. "To suggest," McGregor (p. 63) goes on, "even in a roundabout fashion, that a manager's style is inadequate tends to be threatening. The reasons are obvious if we realize how deeply rooted his style is in his fundamental beliefs, his values, his perception of himself, and his lifetime of experience."

The last of the complex skills I shall mention is as hard to get hold of as "style" and as likely to be misunderstood. I refer to skills necessary to being or acting as a keeper of conscience as well as a manager of affairs. There is or can be a spiritual aspect to administration, as there is or can be to any human pursuit. An individual can be motivated to become an administrator as much by idealism as by opportunities for material gain. From an idealistic base, an administrator may work to identify and communicate the group's ideals and to bring them out in ways visible and satisfying to all.

Appeals to conscience and the addressing of ideals tend to vagueness. Nevertheless, an administrator has some responsibility for being at the moral center of the people and purposes he or she serves. Hesburgh (1971, pp. 763–765) has made this an imperative for presidents. He writes: "While the community is primarily academic, I submit once more that its basis of unity must be of the heart, as well as of the head. . . . The mystique of leadership, be it educational, political, religious, commercial, or whatever, is next to impossible to describe, but wherever it exists, morale flourishes, people pull together towards common goals, spirits soar, order is maintained, not as an end in itself, but as a means to move forward together. Such leadership always has a moral as well as an intellectual dimension; it requires courage as well as wisdom; it does not simply know, it cares."

As to my own intent, I mean this: that one person, having some power vested in him or her by the institution, some central functions of keeping things running smoothly, must also be the one to consciously articulate what that power is for, why educational institutions run at all. It might not be so if one were administering a crude or trivial enterprise, strip mining or the fast food industry, as examples. And yet, just this week I listened to an articulate man, manager of a phosphorus mining operation, defend the despoiling of much of central Florida because out of the despoiled ground in Florida came the fertilizer to make the land green somewhere else to feed the world's hungry millions. It was not a very sophisticated argument, and too much depended upon phrases that had become formulaic through repetition—on about the level of an average college president extolling a college's purposes—but it was made forcefully and clearly as an accepted administrative responsibility. Whatever kind of fertilizer one is selling, then, the responsibility is there for administrators both to justify and enhance the enterprise. In simpler terms, the administrator, in a variety of ways—words, actions, attitudes, and gestures—must perceive and articulate purposes, must be both an inciter to right action and a counterforce to wrong.

The ways are commonplace. The will to find or employ ways is often lacking—and, sometimes, even the realization that an administrator should try to articulate an institution's highest purposes. I shall not try to persuade reluctant administrators other than to say that (1) to some degree the survival of healthy institutions of higher education depends on being able to convince the public of its worth, (2) the importance of education to human survival resides as much in its social and spiritual dimensions as in the material accomplishments it fosters, and (3) administrators are in the key positions to declare and define education's values and hold to living by them.

I do not argue for exclusiveness here: no one else author-ized to have or declare a conscience. Quite the contrary. As admin-istrators discharge this responsibility well, so are they likely to swell the numbers of those who join in the chorus and find their own individual ways of declaring the worth of what they do. At the University of Wisconsin-Oshkosh, a brass plaque commemorates its past history. Begun in 1872 as a normal school, it, like the majority of American universities, has pursued a respectable but modest career. "The University continues to prepare students," the plaque declares, "for the work which George S. Albee, its first president, defined as dedicated to lifting humanity to a higher, nobler life."

Much of what I have argued that administrators should be and do, but in earlier chapters kept closely tied to the more tangible daily operations, applies here. College administrators need to be articulate and literate. The decades—centuries—of rhetoric about high purposes that preceded them should not deter them from striving for noble utterance now. Or, if not that, clear and forceful speaking and writing about the fundamental questions of why learn at all, why insist that human development be other than what chance might make it. How often and to whom and when to exhort and when to show restraint are always to be weighed, but not as excuses to put off or dodge this basic responsibility.

Nor will letting others do it suffice. There is a kind of inner paralysis that grips many institutions. The words and gestures seem all to be directed outward, into catalogue announcements and pro-gram brochures and funding appeals. And as institutions have grown in size, even the definitions customarily found in the official catalogues have shrunk. Worse than the austerity that has come upon publications is an austerity with regard to anything but hard-core information in the internal dialogue of the university. At a Danforth conference five years ago, Harvard's president Derek Bok was an invited major speaker. His remarks and the theme of the conference concerned the loss of and need for community, not just in higher education institutions but in modern society. They were good remarks, their substance doubtless brought forth before and to be brought forth again, though obviously not before the Harvard faculty. They were also new, in the way all individual utterances on vital matters are both clichés and new. The individual in this instance was the president of the most respected university in the country. And yet, not quite as an offhand remark, he said he would not be addressing the Harvard faculty in this way, implying that they were unaddressable. He was making a humorous remark, one accepted by most of the audience, delighted by a confession of presidential impotency and a reaffirmation of faculty power. But the readiness with which the remark came forth and the accepted truth of the situation behind it, hint at serious lacks. Why should not a Derek Bok address the Harvard faculty, harangue them even, spur them to examine their individual and collective consciences? Why should not the Harvard faculty listen, be affirmed or aroused to rejoinder? Why should not every president have the inner strength, the moral center matched with the kind of wisdom and experience that is different from, neither inferior nor superior to, the faculty's, to be a visible and vocal presence before faculty and students as well as donors and trustees? Why should deans so shrink from addressing themselves to values? Why should so many department chairpersons conceive of themselves as managers of things rather than shapers of destiny?

Big words? Vain words? Embarrassing words? Yes and no. Henry Adams, as tired and cynical and yet doggedly valuing as he often is, is right. Teachers affect eternity. And administrators must give over some of their time to living in eternity and facing up to the demands, not of calendar and budget and the crowd below and the powers above, but of the universe. And if, at this book's end, they find the message vague, the rhetoric embarrassing, can't figure out where to go to put in the call or what line to take it on, then they'd best shut down the office for a time, disconnect themselves from the university altogether, and put themselves in some communication with the universe. The university will be there when they get back, waiting for, hoping for, depending upon, whatever it is they have heard.

References

ADAIR, J. *Action-Centered Leadership*. Berkshire, England: Mc-Graw-Hill, 1973.

American Association of University Professors. "Statement on Faculty Workload." *AAUP Bulletin*, 1970, *56*, 30–32.

ARGYRIS, C. *Personality and Organization: The Conflict Between System and the Individual*. New York: Harper & Row, 1957.

ARGYRIS, C. *Management and Organizational Development: The Path from XA to YB*. New York: McGraw-Hill, 1971.

ASTIN, H. S., and BAYER, A. E. "Sex Discrimination in Academe." *Educational Record*, 1972, *53*, 101–118.

BALDERSTON, F. E. *Managing Today's University*. San Francisco: Jossey-Bass, 1974.

BASIL, D. C. *Women in Management*. New York: Dunellen, 1972.

BENNIS, W. G. "Leadership Theory and Administrative Behavior: The Problem of Authority." *Administrative Science Quarterly*, 1959, *4*, 259–301.

BENNIS, W. G. *Organization Development: Its Nature, Origins, and Prospects*. Reading, Mass.: Addison-Wesley, 1969.

BENNIS, W. G. "An O.D. Expert in the Cat Bird's Seat." *Journal of Higher Education*, 1973, *44*, 389–398.

BERNARD, J. *Academic Women*. University Park: Pennsylvania State University Press, 1964.

BERNSTEIN, J. "Biology Watcher." *The New Yorker*, Jan. 2, 1978, pp. 27–46.

150

BIRD, C. *Social Psychology*. New York: Appleton-Century-Crofts, 1940.

BLACKWELL, T. E. *College and University Administration*. New York: Center for Applied Research in Education, 1966.

BOLTON, C. K., and BOYER, R. K. "Organizational Development for Academic Departments." *Journal of Higher Education,* 1973, *44*, 352–369.

BOLTON, E. C., and GENCK, F. H. "Universities and Management." *Journal of Higher Education,* 1971, *42*, 279–291.

BRANN, J., and EMMET, T. A. (Eds.). *The Academic Department or Division Chairman: A Complex Role.* Detroit: Balamp, 1972.

BUTLER, B. N. "Higher Education's Leadership in the Nation's Third Century." *Educational Record,* 1976, *57*, 53–57.

CAFFREY, J. and MOSMANN, C. J. *Computers on Campus.* Washington, D.C.: American Council on Education, 1967.

Carnegie Commission on Higher Education. *The More Effective Use of Resources.* New York: McGraw-Hill, 1972.

Carnegie Commission on Higher Education. *Governance of Higher Education: A Report and Recommendations.* New York: McGraw-Hill, 1973a.

Carnegie Commission on Higher Education. *Opportunities for Women in Higher Education.* New York: McGraw-Hill, 1973b.

CAWS, P., RIPLEY, S. D., and RITTERBUSH, P. C. *The Bankruptcy of Academic Policy.* Washington, D.C.: Acropolis Books, 1972.

CHALMERS, E. L., JR. "Achieving Equity for Women in Higher Education Graduate Enrollment and Faculty Status." *Journal of Higher Education,* 1972, *43*, 517–524.

CHURCHMAN, C. W. *Challenge to Reason.* New York: McGraw-Hill, 1968.

COHEN, M. D., and MARCH, J. G. *Leadership and Ambiguity: The American College President.* New York: McGraw-Hill, 1973.

CONRAD, J. *The Nigger of the "Narcissus."* New York: Harper & Row, 1951.

CORBALLY, J. E. "Evaluation of Administrator Performance." Faculty Letter No. 239. University of Illinois, September 6, 1973.

CORSON, J. J. *Governance of Colleges and Universities.* New York: McGraw-Hill, 1960.

CRAVEN, E. C. "Information Decision Systems in Higher Education:

A Conceptual Framework." *Journal of Higher Education,* 1975, *46,* 125–139.

DEMERATH, N. J., STEPHENS, R. W., and TAYLOR, R. R. *Power, Presidents, and Professors.* New York: Basic Books, 1967.

DIBDEN, A. J. (Ed.). *The Academic Deanship in American Colleges and Universities.* Carbondale and Edwardsville: Southern Illinois University Press, 1968.

DOBBINS, C. G., and STAUFFER, T. M. "Academic Administrators— Born or Made?" *Educational Record,* 1972, *53,* 293–299.

DODDS, H. W. *The Academic President—Educator or Caretaker?* New York: McGraw-Hill, 1962.

DRESCH, S. P. "A Critique of Planning Models for Postsecondary Education: Current Feasibility, Potential Relevance, and a Prospectus for Future Research." *Journal of Higher Education,* 1975, *46,* 245–286.

DRESSEL, P. L., JOHNSON, F. C., and MARCUS, P. M. *The Confidence Crisis: An Analysis of University Departments.* San Francisco: Jossey-Bass, 1970.

DRUCKER, P. "How to Manage Your Time: Everybody's No. 1 Problem." *Harper's,* December, 1966, pp. 56–60.

DRUCKER, P. *The Effective Executive.* New York: Harper & Row, 1967.

DRUCKER, P. *Technology, Management, and Society.* New York: Harper & Row, 1970.

EBLE, K. E. *Professors as Teachers.* San Francisco: Jossey-Bass, 1972.

EBLE, K. E. *The Craft of Teaching: A Guide to Mastering the Professor's Art.* San Francisco: Jossey-Bass, 1976.

EELLS, W. C., and HOLLIS, E. V. *Administration of Higher Education: An Annotated Bibliography.* Washington, D.C.: Office of Education, 1960.

EELLS, W. C., and HOLLIS, E. V. *The College Presidency 1900– 1960: An Annotated Bibliography.* Washington, D.C.: Office of Education, 1961.

EHRLE, E. B. "Selection and Evaluation of Department Chairmen." *Educational Record,* 1975, *56,* 29–38.

EWING, D. W. (Ed.). *Long-Range Planning for Management.* New York: Harper & Row, 1972.

FELTNER, B. D. "Training Programs for College Administrators: Impact on Governance." *Educational Record*, 1975, *56*, 156–159.

FERRARI, M. R. *Profiles of American College Presidents.* East Lansing: Michigan State University Business Studies, 1970.

FULLER, B. "A Framework for Academic Planning." *Journal of Higher Education*, 1976, *47*, 65–77.

GAFF, S. S., FESTA, C., and GAFF, J. G. *Professional Development: A Guide to Resources.* New Rochelle, N.Y.: Change Magazine Press, 1978.

GIBB, C. A. (Ed.). *Leadership: Selected Readings.* New York: Penguin Books, 1969.

GOERSS, K. V. W. *Women Administrators in Education: A Review of Research 1960–1976.* Washington, D.C.: National Association for Women Deans, Administrators, and Counselors, 1977.

GORDON, F. E., and STROBER, M. *Bringing Women into Management.* New York: McGraw-Hill, 1975.

GOULD, J. W. *The Academic Deanship.* New York: Teachers College, Columbia University, 1964.

GOULDNER, A. (Ed.). *Studies in Leadership.* New York: Harper & Row, 1950.

GREENLEAF, R. K. *Servant Leadership.* New York: Paulist Press, 1977.

GRUMBACH, D. "The Demise of the Yellow Card." *The Chronicle of Higher Education*, Feb. 7, 1977, p. 32.

GUBASTA, J. L., and KAUFMAN, N. "Developing Information for Academic Management: An Alternative to Computer-Based Systems." *Journal of Higher Education*, 1977, *48*, 401–411.

HARE, A. P., BORGATTA, E. F., and BALES, R. F. (Eds.). *Small Groups: Studies in Social Interaction.* New York: Knopf, 1965.

HENDERSON, A. D. "Finding and Training Academic Administrators." *Public Administration Review*, 1960, *20*, 17–22.

HENDERSON, A. D. *Training University Administrators: A Programme Guide.* Paris: United Nations Educational, Scientific, and Cultural Organization, 1970.

HENNIG, M., and JARDIM, A. *The Managerial Woman.* New York: Doubleday, 1977.

HERZBERG, F. *The Managerial Choice: To Be Efficient and To Be Human.* Homewood, Ill.: Dow Jones-Irwin, 1976.

154   References

HESBURGH, T. M. "Presidential Leadership." *Journal of Higher Education,* 1971, *42,* 763–765.

HILL, W. W., and FRENCH, W. L. "Perceptions of Power of Department Chairmen by Professors." *Administrative Science Quarterly,* 1967, *2,* 548–574.

IRWIN, J. T. (Ed.). *A Guide to Professional Development Opportunities for College and University Administrators.* Washington, D.C.: Academy for Educational Development and American Council on Education, 1975.

JONES, M. H. *Executive Decision Making.* Homewood, Ill.: Dow Jones-Irwin, 1957.

Journal of the National Association of Women Deans, Administrators, and Counselors. *Women in Administration.* Parts I and II, 1975, *38.*

KAUFFMAN, J. *The Selection of College and University Presidents.* Washington, D.C.: Association of American Colleges, 1974.

KEANE, G. F. "Strengthening College Administration." *Management Controls,* 1970, *17,* 56–61.

KNAPP, P. H. (Ed.). *The Expression of the Emotions in Man.* New York: International Universities Press, 1963.

KNOWLES, A. S. (Ed.). *Handbook of College and University Administration.* Vols. 1 and 2. New York: McGraw-Hill, 1970.

KOLSTOE, O. P. *College Professoring.* Carbondale and Edwardsville: Southern Illinois University Press, 1975.

KUTTNER, M. S. "Managing for Clerical Efficiency." *Management Controls,* 1970, *17,* 10–13.

LAHTI, R. E. *Innovative College Management: Implementing Proven Organizational Practice.* San Francisco: Jossey-Bass, 1973.

LESLIE, D. W. "The Status of the Department Chairmanship in University Organization." *AAUP Bulletin,* 1973, *59,* 419–426.

LEVINSON, H. *The Exceptional Executive: A Psychological Conception.* Cambridge: Harvard University Press, 1968.

LEVINSON, H. *Executive Stress.* New York: Harper & Row, 1974.

LIKERT, R. *The Human Organization: Its Management and Value.* New York: McGraw-Hill, 1967.

LUFT, J. *Group Processes.* Palo Alto, Calif.: National Press, 1962.

MC CLELLAND, D. C. *Power: The Inner Experience.* New York: Irvington, 1975.

MC GREGOR, D. *The Human Side of Enterprise.* New York: McGraw-Hill, 1960.

MC GREGOR, D. *The Professional Manager.* New York: McGraw-Hill, 1967.

MC HENRY, D. E., and ASSOCIATES. *Academic Departments: Problems, Variations, and Alternatives.* San Francisco: Jossey-Bass, 1977.

MACHIAVELLI, N. *The Prince* and *The Discourses.* New York: Random House Modern Library, 1940.

MC INTOSH, E., and MAIER, R. "Management Skills in a Changing Academic Environment." *Educational Record,* 1976, *57,* 87–91.

MC KEACHIE, W. J. "Memo to a New Department Chairman." *Educational Record,* 1968, *49,* 221–227.

MARSHALL, M. "How to Be a Dean." *AAUP Bulletin,* 1956, *42,* 636–643.

MAUER, G. J. (Ed.). *Crisis in Campus Management: Case Studies in the Administration of Colleges and Universities.* New York: Praeger, 1976.

MILL, J. S. *On Liberty.* New York: Appleton-Century-Crofts, 1947.

MILLETT, J. D. *Decision Making and Administration in Higher Education.* Kent, Ohio: Kent State University Press, 1968.

MILLETT, J. D. "Higher Education Management versus Business Management." *Educational Record,* 1975, *56,* 221–225.

MOSMANN, C. *Academic Computers in Service: Effective Uses for Higher Education.* San Francisco: Jossey-Bass, 1973.

PALOLA, E. G., LEHMANN, T., and BLISCHKE, W. R. *Higher Education by Design: The Sociology of Planning.* Berkeley, Calif.: Center for Research and Development in Higher Education, 1970.

PERKINS, J. A. (Ed.). *The University as an Organization.* New York: McGraw-Hill, 1973.

PHILLIPS, E. L., JR. *A New Approach to Academic Administration.* New York: Teachers College, Columbia University Press, 1969.

PRINCE, G. M. *The Practice of Creativity.* New York: Harper & Row, 1970.

RIM, Y. "How Reliable Are Letters of Recommendation?" *Journal of Higher Education,* 1976, *47,* 437–445.

ROACH, J. H. L. "The Academic Department Chairperson: Functions and Responsibilities." *Educational Record,* 1976, *57,* 13–23.

ROURKE, F. E., and BROOKS, G. E. *The Managerial Revolution in Higher Education.* Baltimore: Johns Hopkins University Press, 1966.

RYAN, D. W. "The Internal Organization of Academic Departments." *Journal of Higher Education,* 1972, *43,* 464–482.

SALMEN, S. *Duties of Administrators in Higher Education.* New York: Macmillan, 1971.

SCHLOSSBERG, N. K. "The Right To Be Wrong Is Gone: Women in Academe." *Educational Record,* 1974, *55,* 257–262.

SELZNICK, P. *Leadership in Administration.* New York: Harper & Row, 1957.

SHUCK, E. C. "The New Planning and an Old Pragmatism." *Journal of Higher Education,* 1977, *48,* 594–602.

SOLMON, L. C., and TIERNEY, M. L. "Determinants of Job Satisfaction Among College Administrators." *Journal of Higher Education,* 1977, *48,* 412–431.

SOMMERFELD, R., and NAGELY, D. "Seek and Ye Shall Find: The Organization and Conduct of a Search Committee." *Journal of Higher Education,* 1974, *45,* 239–252.

SPILKA, M. "Parties and Funerals: An Academic Confession." *College English,* 1974, *35,* 367–380.

STOGDILL, R. M. *Handbook of Leadership.* New York: Free Press, 1974.

STOKE, H. W. *The American College President.* New York: Harper & Row, 1959.

STROUP, H. *Bureaucracy in Higher Education.* New York: Free Press, 1966.

TEAD, O. *The Art of Leadership.* New York: McGraw-Hill, 1935.

TEAD, O. *The Art of Administration.* New York: McGraw-Hill, 1951.

THOREAU, H. D. *Walden.* Boston: Houghton Mifflin, 1957.

WALTZER, H. *The Job of Academic Department Chairman: Experience and Recommendations from Miami University.* Washington, D.C.: American Council on Education, 1975.

Index